An integrated course for communicative success

Wanna Talk

3

INTRODUCTION

Wanna Talk 3 is the third book in the **Wanna Talk** series, a three level course specially designed for beginning through intermediate level students who are studying English as a foreign language. **Wanna Talk 3** gives students more opportunities than other books of its kind to learn English through a diversity of activities. The course combines speaking, listening, reading and writing activities. Students are able to actively participate in meaningful exchanges during pair work and group work. The primary goal of the course is to help students communicate appropriately and effectively according to the situation, purpose and roles of the participants. It is designed to promote language acquisition through student participation in purposeful interaction. Each unit in this book revolves around a practical theme. Each unit contains the following sections.

Get started

This section introduces the principle topic of the unit and stimulates students' interest in the theme of the unit. It presents the unit's frequently used vocabulary in diverse ways.

Talk together

In this section, students will listen to a dialogue and then practice with a partner. The dialogue employs everyday language in a wide range of real-life settings and situations. This section also includes the main language expressions of the unit.

Language focus

This section contains an overview of the sentence structures and key expressions presented in the unit. This provides language models for the students that they can use as a quick reference while doing the exercises.

Practice more

This section provides more opportunities for the students to do drill exercises using the key expressions from the *Language focus* section.

Let's do it 1 & 2

These two sections contain both listening and speaking activities. Students can practice more conversational functions and strategies based on the key expressions and topic of the unit. It aims to build students' confidence in communicative situations. Moreover, pair work and group work activities help students expand on what they have learned and use the language for meaningful and free speaking practice.

CONTENTS

- Introduction — 2
- Scope and Sequence — 4

  - **UNIT 01** What is she like? — 7
  - **UNIT 02** What did you use to do when you were younger? — 15
  - **UNIT 03** What do you do to stay in shape? — 23
  - **UNIT 04** What do you do when you're bored? — 31
  - **UNIT 05** Have you ever gone bungee jumping? — 39
  - **UNIT 06** What's the purpose of your trip? — 47
  - **UNIT 07** Could you get me some water? — 55
  - **UNIT 08** While you are on vacation, what will you do? — 63
  - **UNIT 09** What is your ideal type? — 71
  - **UNIT 10** If you won the lottery, what would you do? — 79
  - **UNIT 11** Could you tell me the way to the bank? — 87
  - **UNIT 12** Where do you go to school? — 95

- Listening Script — 103

Reading

The reading section exposes students to a wide variety of authentic and topic related content. Therefore, students can expand their real life knowledge and develop their ability to use that knowledge in the topic related communication. This section also helps students develop critical thinking skills and inferencing skills.

Writing

The *Writing* section helps students to enhance their writing skills with a variety of short writing tasks. This section helps students relate to what they have learned in the unit through meaningful writing practice. Students are therefore given the chance to express themselves in writing.

SCOPE AND SEQUENCE

Units	Topics	Functions	Grammar
01 What is she like?	• Appearance • Personality	• Asking about and describing people's appearances and personality • Talking about what characteristics of a person determine his / her personality • Describing what someone is wearing	• Simple present: *Wh-* questions and statements • Adjectives for describing people's looks and personality
02 What did you use to do when you were younger?	• Personal history • Childhood activities • Past events • Past habits	• Talking about personal history • Talking about favorite activities in the past • Describing habitual activities in the past • Talking about school life in the past	• Simple past: *Wh-* questions and statements • *Used to* for past habits • Past forms of regular / irregular verbs
03 What do you do to stay in shape?	• Health • Diet • Exercises • Body shape • Fitness	• Talking about staying in shape • Talking about eating habits and doing exercises • Giving advice on how to stay healthy • Talking about frequency of activities	• Verb + to-inf. • Verb + gerund • *How often...?* • *How many times a week...?* • Frequency expressions
04 What do you do when you're bored?	• Feelings • Emotions • Advice	• Asking about and describing feelings and emotions • Talking about the reasons that cause certain feelings • Talking about the activities people do when they are in certain moods. • Giving advice on getting rid of negative feelings	• Simple present: *Wh-* questions • Adverbial clauses: *because... when...* • Adjectives for describing feelings and emotions

Units	Topics	Functions	Grammar
05 **Have you ever gone bungee jumping?**	• Past experiences and events	• Talking about past experiences and events • Asking about and telling how long one has been doing a certain activity • Talking about the most memorable experience in one's life	• Present perfect: *Have you + p.p...?* • Present perfect progressive: *How long have you been + ~ing?* • *Go + ~ing*
06 **What's the purpose of your trip?**	• Travel • Airport: Immigration • Hotel: Services and facilities • Itinerary	• Reserving a flight • Going though immigration • Reserving a hotel room • Asking for hotel services • Talking about travel plans and itineraries • Talking about vacation activities • Describing types of trips • Writing emails about one's travels	• Simple present: *Wh-* questions • Future progressive: *Wh-* questions • *Would like to* + verb
07 **Could you get me some water?**	• Requests • Permission	• Making requests • Accepting or refusing requests • Asking for permission • Giving and declining permission • Telling reasons for declining requests and permission	• *Can, Could, Would, Would you mind + ~ing* for making requests • *May, Would you mind if...?, Is it OK if...?* for asking for permission
08 **While you are on vacation, what will you do?**	• Free time activities • Future plans • Invitations • Time off	• Talking about favorite free time activities and future plans • Talking about activities one will do in a certain situation in the future • Making invitations • Accepting and refusing invitations	• Time clauses • Subordinating conjunctions: *when, if, while, before, after, as soon as* • *How(What) about...?, Would you like to...?, Why don't we...?* for making invitations

SCOPE AND SEQUENCE

Units	Topics	Functions	Grammar
09 What is your ideal type?	• Dating • Friendship • Ideal type	• Talking about relationships between men and women • Talking about the qualities of a good friend • Describing one's ideal type of man and woman	• Simple present: *Wh*-questions • Adjective clause: *someone who...* • Adjectives for describing one's qualities
10 If you won the lottery, what would you do?	• Hypothetical situations • Suggestions	• Talking about imaginary situations • Talking about wishes and dreams • Asking for and giving suggestions	• Unreal conditional
11 Could you tell me the way to the bank?	• Locations of places • Directions • Distance	• Talking about locations of places • Asking for and giving directions to places • Asking and answering about the distance to a place • Asking for and making recommendations	• Prepositions of places • Imperatives • *Is there...?* • Indirect questions: *Could you tell me where...?* • *How far...?* • *How long does it take...?*
12 Where do you go to school?	• Education • School subjects • College majors	• Talking about various fields of study • Talking about how to register for courses in college • Talking about kinds of schools and degrees or diplomas • Talking about educational systems in different countries • Talking about plans regarding education	• Simple present: *Wh-* questions • Future form: *What do you want to...?*

01 What is she like?

Lesson Focus

01 Asking about and describing people's appearances and personality
02 Talking about what characteristics of a person determine his / her personality
03 Describing what someone is wearing
04 Using adjectives to describe people's looks and personality

UNIT 01 What is she like?

Get started

A. What does each of these people look like? Try to write proper words to describe each person. Then discuss the questions below with your partner.

Amanda	Tony
Height:	Height:
Build:	Build:
Hair:	Hair:

Lisa	Scott
Height:	Height:
Build:	Build:
Hair:	Hair:

1. Who do you think is in the best shape?
2. Who is of average height and weight?
3. Who is short with a medium build?
4. Who is big and chubby?

B. Choose the proper word that describes each person's personality. Then with your partner, talk about what each person is like. Follow the example.

Sarah's friends trust her so much. They tell her their secrets.   •   • outgoing

Wendy always thinks she is right and others are wrong. She doesn't like to change her opinion.   •   • selfish

Peter likes to party and enjoys hanging out with friends.   •   • adventurous

Sean only thinks of himself. He doesn't care about other people.   •   • reliable

Jamie likes to try challenging new sports and learning new things.   •   • conservative

Jody is a traditional thinker and doesn't like change.   •   • narrow-minded

Example

A: What's Sarah like?

B: Oh, she is reliable. Her friends trust her so much. They tell her their secrets.

Talk together 🎧

Listen to the dialogue and practice.

Jasmine: Hi, Nick. How are things going?

Nick: Not bad. How about you?

Jasmine: I'm fine. Well, I met one of my college friends yesterday, and she told me that she wants to meet a new guy. I know you don't have a girlfriend. Are you interested in a blind date? She's about your age and is a jewelry designer.

Nick: Umm... before I say OK... what does she look like?

Jasmine: Well... she's average height and quite slim. She has long straight hair.

Nick: What is she like? Is she outgoing?

Jasmine: Yes, she is. She is also friendly and smart. I am sure you two will get along well with each other.

Nick: Great! I look forward to meeting her. Let's arrange the date.

Language focus

What does s/he look like?

Age	She's in her early/mid/late 20s. He is young/middle-aged/old.	**Hair**	She has short, medium-length, long,	straight, wavy, curly,	brown, hair. black blond(e)
Height	He is tall/short/average height.		He is bald. He has a beard / a mustache / sideburns.		
Build	He's thin/well-built/overweight. She's slim/average weight/ plump/chubby.				

What's s/he like?

He is smart, outgoing and humorous.
She's friendly, naive and shy.
He is my favorite teacher and is generous and nice.

Practice more

A. With your partner, talk about the appearance of each person in the picture. Use the words given below. Follow the example.

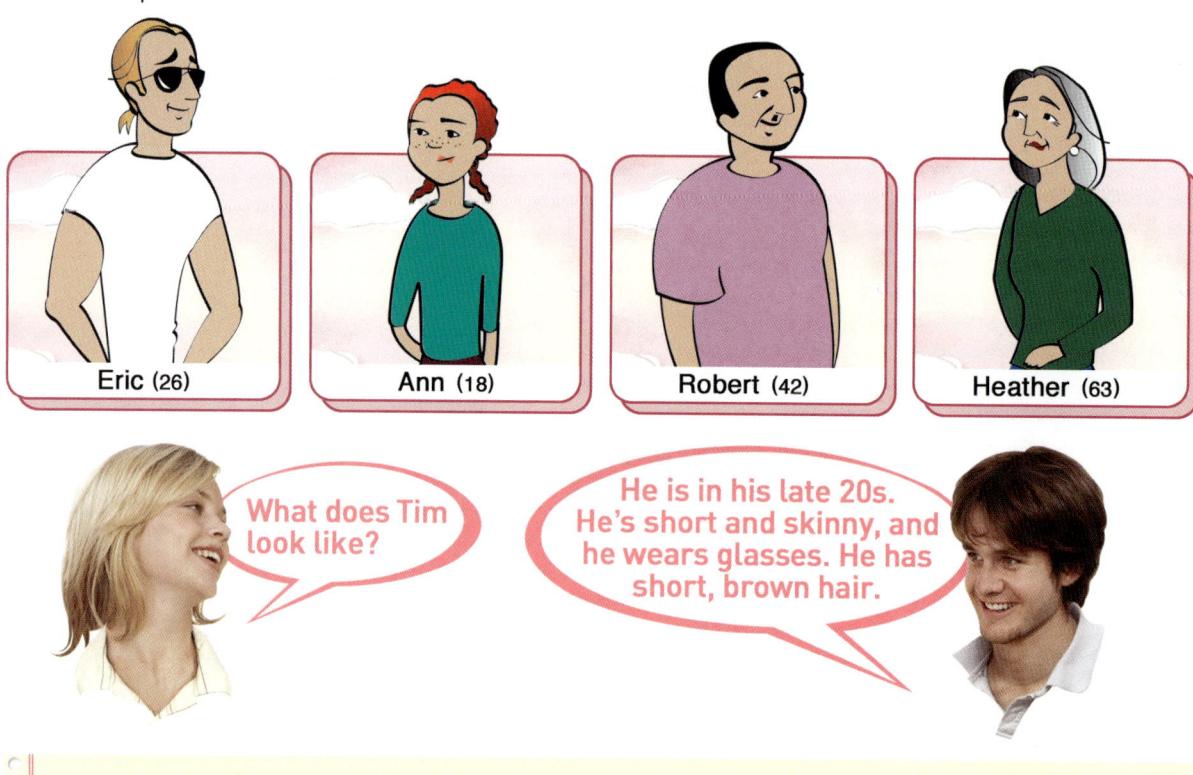

wears sunglasses	is muscular
has wrinkles around his / her eyes	is chubby
has freckles on his / her cheeks	has a mustache
wears his / her hair in a ponytail	wears his / her hair in braids

B. Choose the proper word that describes each person's personality. Then with your partner, talk about what each person is like. Follow the example.

Name	Personalities

- active
- outgoing
- reliable
- hardworking
- humorous
- responsible
- generous
- friendly
- honest
- smart
- shy
- cheerful
- flexible
- talkative

What's Julie like?

Oh, she is friendly, reliable, and smart.

Let's do it 1 🎧

A. Austin and Sarah are friends from back in high school. They are looking at their school yearbook while thinking back on the good old days. Listen to the conversation and label each person with his / her name.

B. Listen again and write down the words that describe the appearance of each person in the conversation.

Tyler

Nick

Melissa

Nicole

Kevin

C. With your partner, take turns describing someone and drawing the person being described. Describe the appearance of someone from your family or one of your friends to your partner. Then see if your partner draws the person in the same way as you described. See the example.

> **Example**
>
> My sister is in her early 20s. She is a university student. She is quite tall and of average build. She has shoulder-length, dark brown hair in braids. She has short bangs as well. She has big eyes and thin lips. Oh, and she likes to wear a mini skirt.

What is she like? • 11

Let's do it 2

A. Try to think about the people you know who have the following personality traits. Then write their names under the proper headings.

Someone who is strict and conservative	Someone who is sociable and humorous	Someone who is smart and open-minded	Someone who is reliable and generous

B. Listen to the descriptions of four people and fill in the table with the proper words from the list.

Who?	What are they like?

- warm-hearted
- cheerful
- flexible
- brave
- humorous
- honest
- polite
- strict
- intelligent
- hardworking
- reliable
- challenging

C. Choose three of the people you wrote down in Part **A** and write their names in the table below. Then fill in the table with the descriptions of their personalities. After you are done with this table, take turns with your partner describing the people. You may use the words given below.

	Name	Personalities	The reason she / he is...
1			
2			
3			

- **strict and conservative** → never allows me to come home late or wear a mini skirt, gives a 10 pm curfew
- **sociable and humorous** → likes partying and hanging out with people, knows many jokes
- **smart and open-minded** → top student of the class, listens to other people's opinions
- **reliable and generous** → likes to work with other people, likes to help and take care of other people

Example

A: I am going to tell you about my friend, Michelle.
She is smart and open-minded. She is going to medical school to become a doctor.
Also, she always listens to other people's opinions.

B: Oh! Sounds like she is a really smart and open-minded person.

Reading

A. What do you look like? What are you like? Decide if you're the right person for the positions in the wanted ads posted on a school bulletin board.

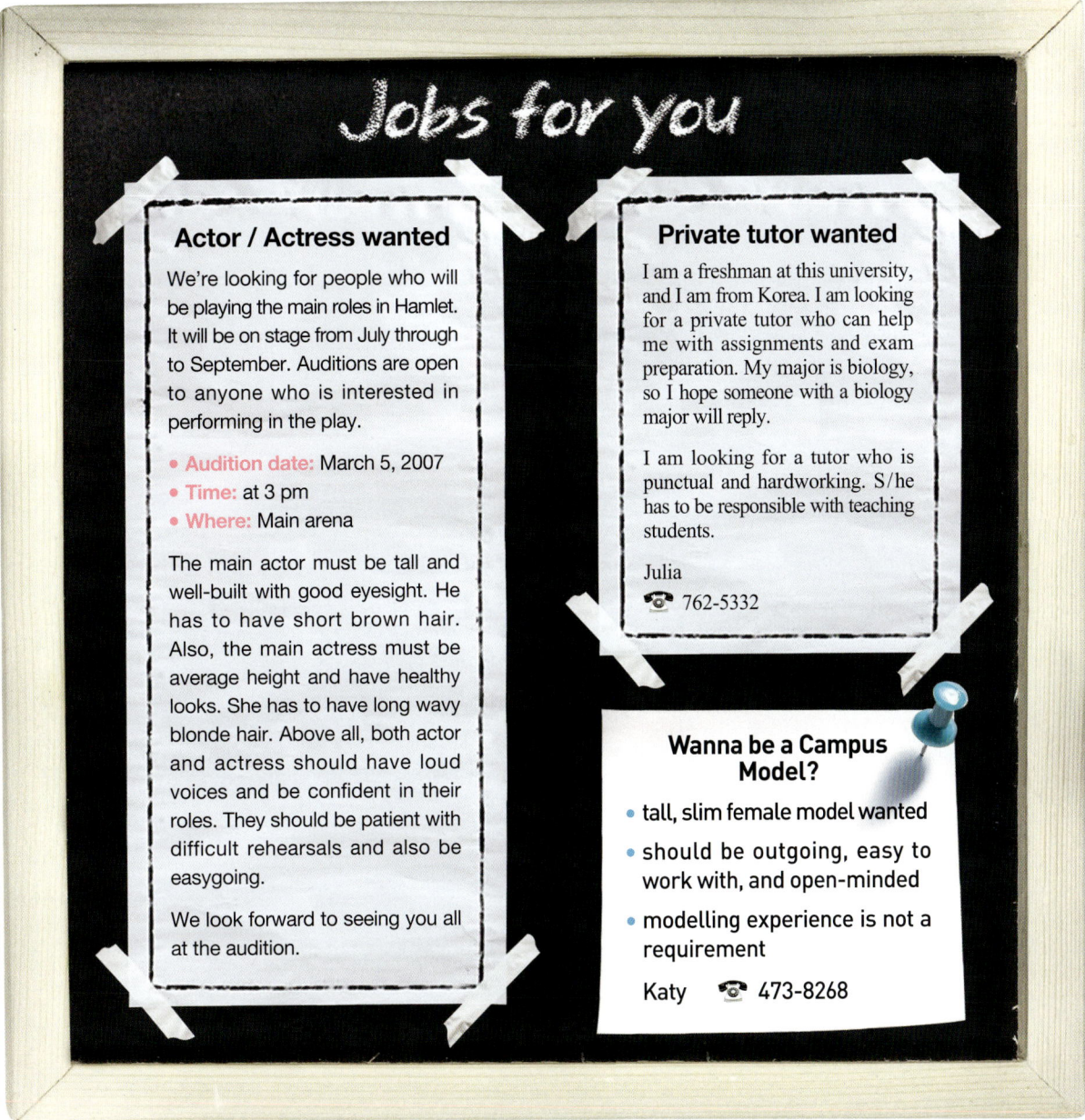

B. Discuss these questions with your partner.

1. If you're looking for a new job, what kind of position are you looking for? And why do you think you are good for the position?

2. Would you like to take part in the audition in the want-ads? If yes, why do you think you would be good for that role? If not, why not?

3. Would you like to apply as a private tutor? If yes, why do you think you suit that position? If not, why not?

4. Would you like to be a campus model? If yes, why do you think you're good for that position? If not, why not?

Writing

A. When you think of the people around you and those you've met before, can you describe what they are like? Choose one of the topics below and brainstorm your ideas to describe the person. Then write a short passage about him / her based on the words you wrote down when brainstorming. Use the example as a guide.

❶ Describe an unforgettable teacher

❷ Describe your best friend

❸ Describe one of your classmates or co-workers.

❹ Describe your boy / girlfriend or spouse.

Example

Brainstorming

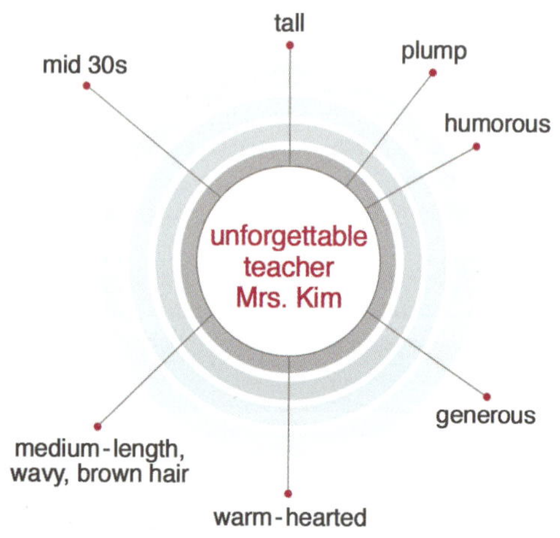

- tall
- mid 30s
- plump
- humorous
- generous
- warm-hearted
- medium-length, wavy, brown hair

(center: unforgettable teacher Mrs. Kim)

An unforgettable teacher

I'll never forget Mrs. Kim, who was my high school teacher. She was in her mid 30s at that time. She was tall, a little bit plump and had a medium-length, wavy, brown hair. She was beautiful. Also, she was generous and humorous. She always told us jokes in the afternoon classes, because students got tired after lunch. She cared about the students who had problems and tried to help them. She understood her students very well and always helped us do the right thing.

Brainstorming

02 What did you use to do when you were younger?

Lesson Focus

- **01** Talking about personal history
- **02** Describing habitual activities in the past
- **03** Talking about favorite activities and school life in the past
- **04** Using *used to* to talk about past habits

UNIT 02
What did you use to do when you were younger?

Get started

A. Read the short histories of three people below. Then discuss the questions that follow with your partner.

❶ Hi, I'm Sam. I'm an English teacher in Korea. I was born in New Zealand but grew up in Sydney, Australia. I studied English in college. I came to Korea in 2006 to teach English and to learn about Korean culture. Now, I am working at a language school in Korea.

❷ I'm Lucy. Our family lived in New York when I was a kid. So I went to many musicals with my parents and wanted to be a musical actress. Thirteen years later, I debuted in Cats in New York. I'm one of the most popular actresses in New York and London.

❸ Hi, my name is Steve. I live in San Diego. Our family moved to the States from Mexico when I was 10. I started working as a part-time bartender when I was in high school. After high school, I got a job at a fancy bar and kept saving money. Now, I run my own restaurant.

❶ Where were these people born or where did they grow up?
❷ How did they get to where they are now?
❸ Give your partner a brief personal history about yourself like the ones above.

B. What were the things you liked to do during the following periods? Use the words in the list if needed, but try to use your own words as well.

What did you like to do...	
when you were a kid?	
when you were in your teens?	
when you were a university student?	

- play with dolls
- read books
- make model cars
- play hide and seek
- play video(computer) games
- play the piano / guitar...
- play a lot of sports
- hang out with friends
- go dancing

Talk together

Listen to the dialogue and practice.

George: Don't you miss your high school days?
Lucy: Sometimes. Where did you go to high school?
George: I went to high school in Austin, Texas.
Lucy: Were you born in Texas?
George: Actually, I was born in California and moved to Texas when I was 11.
Lucy: I see. What did you like to do when you were a teenager?
George: I was crazy about rock music, so I collected a lot of CDs.
Lucy: I did too. I have about 100 CDs at home.
Then what did you do after you graduated from high school?
George: I got into St. Louise College and majored in biology.
Lucy: Oh, did you? What did you use to do when you were in college?
George: I used to play the electric guitar in a rock band.
Lucy: Oh, that's why you still play the electric guitar for our company rock band.

Language focus

When were you born?	I was born in 1980.
Where were you born?	I was born in Austin, Texas.
Where did you go to high school?	I went to Orinda High.
	I went to high school in Austin.
What did you like to do when you were a kid?	I liked to play baseball.
What did you use to do when you were in high school?	I used to play in a soccer team.
What did you do after you graduated from high school?	I started working part-time as a cook.
What were you studying while you were in college?	I was studying computer science.

Practice more

A. Work with your partner. Find out about your partner's past by asking the questions below. Write the answers in complete sentences.

Questions	Answers
Where were you born?	I was _____.
Where did you grow up?	I grew up _____.
Where did you go to elementary school?	I went to _____.
What was your favorite subject?	My favorite _____.

B. With your partner, talk about what your teenage days were like. First, make up questions using the given phrases. Then take turns asking and answering the questions.

When you were a teenager, _____?

Sample Answers

1. what did you want to be → I wanted to be a pilot.
2. what did you use to do → I used to play the piano.
3. what did you like to do → I liked to play in a sports team.

C. What did you do after you turned twenty? Talk about what you did with your partner. First, make questions using the given phrases. Then take turns asking and answering the questions.

After you turned twenty, _____?

Sample Answers

1. what did you do → I started working at a travel agency.
2. what did you use to do in your free time → I used to go dancing.
3. what did you enjoy wearing → I enjoyed wearing leggings.

Let's do it 1

A. Think back of these past times in your life. What did you use to do during each of the time periods? Complete the spider webs by using the expressions in the box.

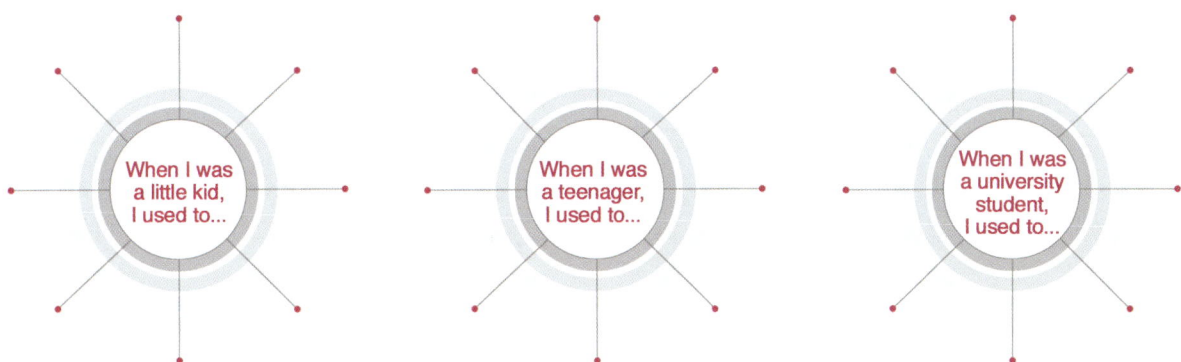

- play with dolls
- read comic books
- get good grades
- be the leader of the class
- have a lot of friends

- play hide and seek
- live in the country
- spend time alone
- get scholarships
- play hockey often

- play a lot of sports
- live in the dorm
- work part time
- play a musical instrument
- play video(computer) games

B. People are talking about the things they used to do. Listen to three conversations. Then put the number of the conversation next to the correct activity.

☐ play baseball   ☐ listen to jazz   ☐ enjoy nights out
☐ read comic books ☐ go to the orchestra   ☐ play the violin
☐ go scuba diving   ☐ have pets   ☐ go camping

C. Talk to your partner about what you liked to do or what you used to do during each of the time periods in Part **A**. Use the conversations in Part **B** or follow the example below.

> **Example**
>
> **A:** What did you like to do when you were a kid?
>
> **B:** I liked to play with dolls.
> I had many Barbie dolls at home.
> How about you? What did you like to do when you were a kid?
>
> **A:** I liked to play soccer. I practiced every day.
> So, what did you use to do when you were a university student?
>
> **B:** When I was a university student, I majored in astronomy.
> So, I used to look at the stars at the observatory.
> How about you?
>
> **A:** I used to play in a school basketball team. I had a lot of fun then.

What did you use to do when you were younger?

Let's do it 2

A. Imagine you're posting your personal history in your blog. Complete the chart using complete sentences.

My history	
+ Date of Birth	I was born
+ Place of Birth	
+ Things I liked to do when I was a kid	
+ Things I used to do when I was a teenager	
+ Things I did after I graduated from high school	
+ Things I do now	

B. Listen to three TV talk show clips. The host is talking to three guests about their personal histories. Check (✓) if the statements below are True or False.

		True	False
Clip 1	When Kimberly was a teenager, she loved to read comic books.		
	Kimberly was fifteen when she started to write stories.		
	After Kimberly became a successful writer, she wrote more than 50 books.		
Clip 2	When Nick was a college student, he majored in French cuisine.		
	Nick decided to become a chef while he was in France.		
	Nick became famous right after he graduated from university.		
Clip 3	Tim majored in construction when he was in university.		
	While Tim was in university, he started altering clothes.		
	After Tim dropped out of the university, he started his own construction business.		

C. Talk to your partner about your personal histories. Use the information in Part **A** and the listening scripts in Part **B** as a guide. Follow the example below.

Example

A: When were you born?
B: I was born in September, 1980.
A: Where were you born?
B: I was born in Seoul, Korea.
A: What did you like to do when you were a kid?
B: I liked watching cartoons on TV.
A: Oh, I see.
   What did you use to do when you were a teenager?
B: I used to be a member of a soccer team.
A: After high school, what did you do?
B: I studied design in college.
A: What do you do now?
B: I am an interior designer.

Reading

A. Read these life histories put in a magazine.

How I became what I am now

I want to tell you about my respectful parents and myself. I was born in Los Angeles and have lived here all my life. When I was young, I wondered why my brothers and I looked different from my friends at school. I realized why when I turned ten. My parents were born in Korea and they grew up there. They started going out when they were in college. After they graduated, they got married. They were happy, but life wasn't as easy as they thought it would be. So, they decided to move to L.A. They worked really hard to make money by serving food, washing dishes and delivering goods. After two years, they saved up some money. Shortly after that, I was born. Now my parents run a small Korean restaurant in downtown L.A.

The way to success

A lot of people in the world know who Steven Paul Jobs is. Steve used to be the CEO of Pixer and now is the CEO of the Apple company. He is a world-renowned leading figure in both the computer and entertainment industries. Achieving success, however, was a long process for Jobs. He was born in San Francisco in 1955. A week after his birth, he was adopted by the Jobs family. He attended schools in California. He used to go to after-school lectures at the Hewlett-Packard Company, and he was later hired to work for the summer. After high school, he entered Reed College in Oregon. He made a turning point while he was in college. He realized that a college degree had no meaning for him. So, he dropped out of college after only one semester and attended classes such as calligraphy on occasion for personal fulfillment. That helped him a lot later on in his life...

B. With your partner, discuss the questions below.

1. What do you think are the touching parts of these two stories?
2. Do you know anybody who has gone through a difficult past and has become successful? What has the person aicheved?
3. Have there been any turning points in your life? Tell your partner about them.

Writing

A. Choose one of the situations below and write your answers to the questions.

1 If you're over twenty years old, think back on your teenage days.

What was your school life like?	What were you like?
Were you a good student?	What kind of music did you like?
What subjects did you like to study?	Did you like to spend time with friends?
What did you like about your school?	What did you use to do?

2 If you're still in your teens, think back to the days when you were a kid.

What was your school life like?	What were you like?
Were you a good student?	Were you a good child to your parents?
What subjects did you like to study?	What kinds of games did you do with your friends?
Did you like to play with your classmates?	What did you use to do?

B. Now, write about your past based on those answers.

Example

When I was a high school student, I was quite popular. Many girls came to see me during breaks. I really enjoyed my high school days. My favorite subject was P.E, because I liked to play soccer. I still see some of my friends from high school. When I was a teenager, I liked to listen to rock music. Back then, my favorite musician was Bon Jovi. Soccer and popular rock music helped me a lot in getting over difficulties. I also used to play the drums in the school band. But, I stopped playing the drums after I broke my arm during a soccer

03 What do you do to stay in shape?

Lesson Focus

- 01 Talking about staying in shape
- 02 Talking about eating habits and doing exercises
- 03 Giving advice on how to stay healthy
- 04 Using frequency expressions to talk about the frequency of activities
- 05 Using verbs taking *to-inf* and verbs taking the gerund as complements accurately

UNIT 03 — What do you do to stay in shape?

Get started

A. Healthy habits are important for staying healthy. Which of these habits do you have? Check (✓) Yes or No for each of the habits.

Healthy Habits	Yes	No
Exercising regularly		
Getting some rest		
Sleeping more than six hours		
Working regular hours		
Reducing/relieving stress		
Drinking more than six glasses of water a day		
Avoiding fattening foods		
Taking vitamins		

B. Choose the right words to complete the expressions below and write them in the blanks.

- do   • be   • stay   • get   • take   • go

___ in shape   ___ exercise   ___ on a diet

Talk together 🎧

Listen to the dialogue and practice.

Jason: Hey, Tracy. You look awesome in those skinny jeans. Are you on a diet or something?
Kate: Yeah, I've tried a fad diet recently, so I lost some weight.
Jason: Oh, really! So what exactly do you do to stay healthy?
Kate: Well, I try to eat light dinners and go for walks.
Jason: How often do you walk?
Kate: You know, there's a park near my place, so I power walk there every other day.
Jason: Then how much time do you spend walking when you go?
Kate: I walk for more than forty minutes. Nowadays, I feel fit.
Jason: And what do you eat for dinner?
Kate: Just a plate of salad with a grilled chicken breast.
Jason: Good for you. Sounds like you have been trying hard to stay fit.
I should start doing some things to get in shape.

Language focus

Frequency expressions	Verb + to-infinitive

How often do you go jogging?
 How many times a week (month) do you go jogging?
 	
 I go jogging   everyday.
                 every other day.
                 every three days.
                 once a week.
                 twice a week.
                 five times a week.
                 every other week.
                 four times a month.
 	
 I don't exercise at all.
	What do you do to stay in shape?
	 I try to eat light dinners and go for walks.
	
	 What does the doctor advise to do ?
	 His advice is to cut down on fatty foods.
	
	 Verb + gerund
	
	 How much time do you spend walking?
	 I spend about forty minutes walking.

Practice more

A. First, answer the questions with your own information. Check (✓) Yes or No. Then ask your partner the same questions and check (✓) Yes or No with his / her information.

Lifestyle & Habits	me		my partner		
	yes	no	yes	no	How often...
1 Do you (ever) exercise?					
2 Do you eat fruit and vegetables?					
3 Do you go to bed early?					
4 Do you smoke?					
5 Do you drink coffee?					
6 Do you eat junk food or fattening food?					
7 Do you go for regular medical check-ups?					

B. Work with your partner. Based on your partner's answers in the chart above, ask how often he / she does these things. Write down your partner's answers in the blanks.

How often do you exercise?
(How many times a week do you exercise?)

I exercise four times a week.

C. Work with your partner. Practice asking and answering the questions below using the expressions and words in the chart.

What do you do to stay healthy?
What do you do to stay in shape?

I exercise four times a week and I go to bed early.

Let's do it 1

A. Use this fitness quiz to find out how healthy you and your partner are. Take turns with your partner asking and answering the questions. Then, add up the points and tell your partner how fit she/he is.

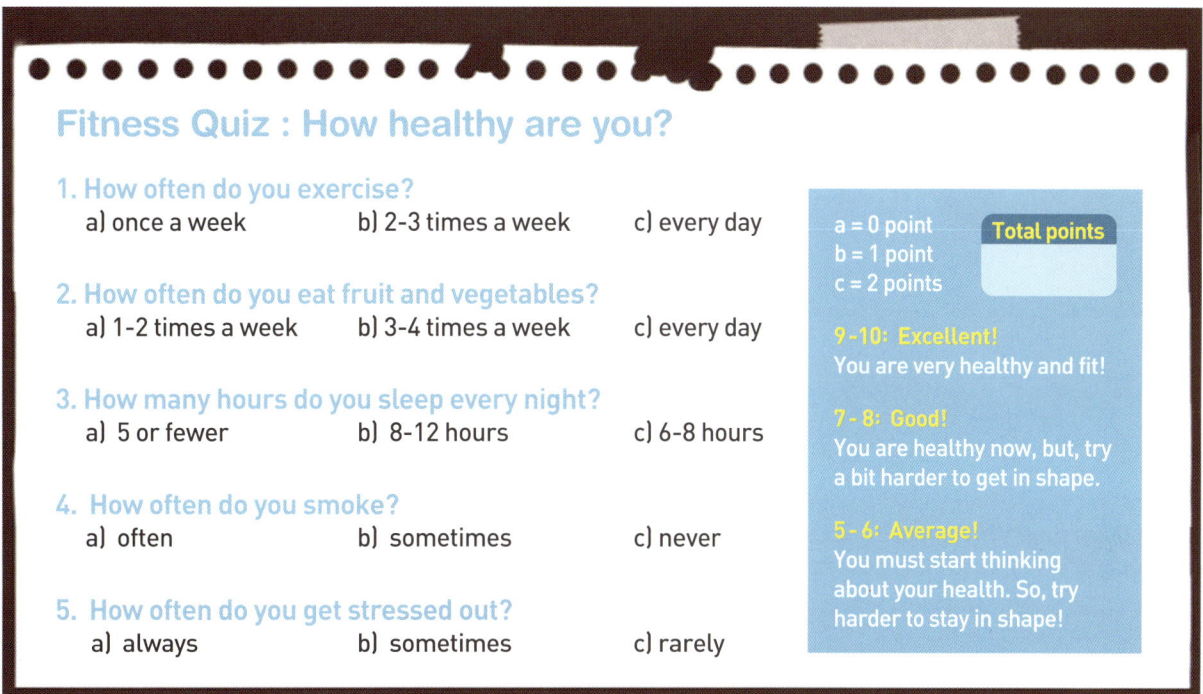

Fitness Quiz : How healthy are you?

1. How often do you exercise?
   a) once a week   b) 2-3 times a week   c) every day

2. How often do you eat fruit and vegetables?
   a) 1-2 times a week b) 3-4 times a week   c) every day

3. How many hours do you sleep every night?
   a) 5 or fewer   b) 8-12 hours   c) 6-8 hours

4. How often do you smoke?
   a) often   b) sometimes   c) never

5. How often do you get stressed out?
   a) always   b) sometimes   c) rarely

a = 0 point
b = 1 point
c = 2 points

Total points

9-10: Excellent!
You are very healthy and fit!

7-8: Good!
You are healthy now, but, try a bit harder to get in shape.

5-6: Average!
You must start thinking about your health. So, try harder to stay in shape!

B. Work in groups of four. Using the Fitness Quiz you did in Part **A**, take turns talking about how healthy you are. Follow the example below.

> **Example**
>
> According to the advice in the fitness quiz, I'm healthy now, but I need to try a bit harder to get in shape.

C. Listen to the conversation between John and Tracy. Complete the sentences about how frequently they do these activities.

John eats junk food
_____
_____

Tracy eats fruit and vegetables
_____
_____

John goes to the gym
_____
_____

Tracy goes jogging
_____
_____

Do you think John is in shape? What about Tracy? Talk to your partner about what advice you'd like to give to them.

Let's do it 2

A. Jesse and Laura are talking about the things they do to stay fit. Listen and fill in the chart with the kinds of exercises they do and the food they eat.

	Exercises	Food
JESSE		
LAURA		

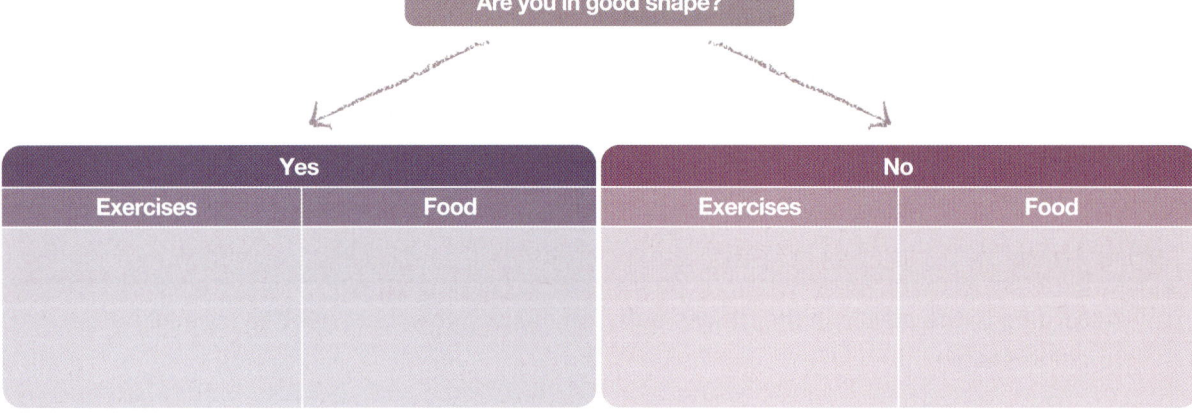

B. Are you in good shape? If you think so, what do you do to stay in shape? What exercises do you do? What kinds of food do you eat? If you don't think so, what would you like to do to get in shape? What exercises would you like to do? What kinds of food would you like to eat? Fill out the chart with your own answers.

Are you in good shape?

Yes		No	
Exercises	Food	Exercises	Food

C. Using the answers above, talk to your partner about what you do to stay fit. Follow the example below.

> **Example**
>
> A: What do you do to stay in shape? Do you ever exercise?
> B: Yes, I do. I go for walks.
> A: How often (how many times a week) do you go for a walk?
> B: I usually walk every other day.
> A: How much time do you spend walking each time?
> B: Well, I usually spend more than fifty minutes walking at a time.
> A: And what do you eat to stay fit?
> B: I eat a lot of fruits and vegetables everyday.

Reading

A. Below is an article from a health magazine. What does it say about staying in shape?

How to stay healthy

Do you want to know how you could stay healthy?
Here are some tips to help you out.

① Have a healthy lifestyle

To keep in shape, you need to have a healthy lifestyle. Try to maintain healthy habits like eating meals at regular times. Also try to get enough sleep every night.

② Eat and drink well

You need to drink at least six glasses of water a day and eat fresh vegetables and fruits. Eat food that is good for your body and has a lot of vitamins and minerals.

③ Not fattening foods

Try not to eat too many sweets or snacks like cookies. Also avoid foods like potato chips and French fries.

④ Exercise regularly

Exercise for at least 40 minutes at least three times a week. You will look and feel better.

⑤ Be positive & reduce stress

Having a happy and positive attitude is very important for staying in shape. Try to reduce the stress in your life because it's bad for your body.

B. With your partner, talk about the following questions.

① Of the five tips above, which tip are you actually trying hard to keep? For how long?

② Do you think you are healthy? If yes, why? If not, why not?

③ Why do you think instant food is unhealthy?

④ Why do you think a positive attitude makes you healthy?

⑤ Are there any additional tips you want to suggest to your classmates? If yes, what are they?

What do you do to stay in shape? • 29

Writing

A. Write about what you do to stay healthy.

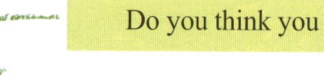
Do you think you are in good shape?

If so, write about what you usually do to stay in shape?

If not, write about what you will do to get in shape.

> **Example**
>
> I think I am in good shape because I exercise regularly. I like doing exercises and I go to the gym six times a week. At the gym, I spend more than fifty minutes exercising. On weekends, I usually go hiking with my family. Also, I try not to eat too many sweets or snacks like ice-cream, chocolate and cookies because they are very fattening. I always try to have a balanced diet and get regular exercise. I don't like drinking coffee, so I drink a lot of water instead.

04 What do you do when you're bored?

Lesson Focus

01 Asking about and describing feelings and emotions
02 Talking about the causes of certain feelings
03 Talking about what people do when they are in certain moods
04 Giving advice on getting rid of negative feelings
05 Using *because* clause to state the reasons of having certain feelings

What do you do when you're bored?

Get started

A. How do these people look? Choose the proper word to describe each picture from the list and write it under the picture.

- excited
- bored
- puzzled
- tired
- surprised
- upset
- depressed
- nervous

B. What makes you feel good? And what makes you feel bad? Match the feelings in the chart with the things that make you feel that way. Try to add your own words.

Feelings	Things that make me feel...	Feelings	Things that make me feel...
excited		surprised	
bored		upset	
puzzled		depressed	
tired		nervous	

- noisy neighbors
- housework / job
- a blind date
- riding roller coasters
- making a speech
- quiet and slow music
- tricky test questions
- unexpected gifts
- working overtime / getting up early

32 • UNIT 04

Talk together

Listen to the dialogue and practice.

Janet: Hey, how's it going?
Ben: I feel so depressed.
Janet: I see. That's why you have a long face. Why is that?
Ben: Maybe it's because it's Monday.
I just don't feel like working on Monday mornings.
Janet: Oh, you might have the 'Monday morning blues.'
As for me, I sometimes feel depressed at work.
Ben: Really? You have never looked tired or depressed at work.
Janet: Maybe you just didn't notice. I have my own way of making myself feel better.
Ben: Oh, what is it? What do you do when you feel depressed?
Janet: When I feel depressed, I go shopping and treat myself to a little gift.
Or I go out for a walk after I get off from work.
Ben: That sounds like a good idea.
Janet: Yeah, I hope you get over the Monday morning blues by finding your own solution, as well.

Language focus

How do you feel? How are you feeling?	I feel tired. I am feeling tired.
Why do you feel tired? When do you feel tired? What makes you tired?	Because I stayed up last night studying for a test. I feel tired when I have too much work to do. Working overtime makes me tired.
What do you do when you feel / get tired?	I usually get some rest at home.

Practice more

A. With your partner, practice the dialogue using the words given below.

Example

A: How do you feel?

B: I feel excited.

A: Why do you feel excited?

B: I feel excited because I got good grades on my final exams.

A: Oh, great.

B: How about you? How are you feeling?

A: Actually, I am feeling tired because I have a lot of work to do.

Feelings & Emotions	Reasons	Feelings & Emotions	Reasons
exhausted	worked over time three days in a row	shocked	got low grades on the final exams
scared	watched horror movies	annoyed	somebody took my sandwiches off my desk
frustrated	left a notebook on the bus	touched	my friends threw me a surprise party

B. With your partner, make dialogues like the example below using the information given in the chart.

Example

A: When do you feel bored?

B: I feel bored when I stay home with nothing to do.

A: Then what do you do when you feel bored?

B: When I feel bored, I go out for a drive. When do you feel tired?

A: I feel tired when I work long hours.

B: Then what do you do when you feel tired?

A: When I feel tired, I go to bed early.

Feelings and Emotions	When…	Things I do…
pleased	I get my work done	I hang out with my friends after work/school.
afraid	I walk home at night	I whistle a song and walk fast.
embarrassed	I fall down on the street	I just look around and run away.
disappointed	my friend lies to me	I talk to my friend face-to-face.
lonely	I'm home alone on the weekend	I chat online.

Let's do it 1

A. Listen to people talking about how they feel now. Choose the proper word from the list that describes how each of them is feeling now.

- guilty
- confused
- confident
- thrilled
- frustrated
- relieved

B. Listen again. Complete the sentences about why they feel that way.

Mike	He feels frustrated because his computer broke down and all the work he did is gone.
Allison	She feels _____ because she _____ to her parents about going _____ with friends.
Claire	She feels _____ because the guy she dated last weekend _____ suddenly.
Tom	He feels _____ because he finally did a _____.
Kenneth	He feels _____ because he thought that he _____ his wallet, but he _____ it back.
Gwen	She feels _____ because she thinks she is _____ for the final _____ and _____.

C. Try to remember the moments you've felt the same way as the people in Part **A**. First, fill in the chart based on your memory. Then with your partner, talk about when and why you felt that way.

I felt	When…	Because…
guilty	My mom called me last Sunday	I didn't remember it was her birthday
confused		
frustrated		
thrilled		
confident		
relieved		

Example

A: When was the last time you felt guilty?
B: I felt guilty when my mom called me last Sunday.
A: Why did you feel guilty?
B: Because I didn't remember it was her birthday.

Let's do it 2

A. How do these people feel? What makes each person feel that way? Complete the sentences below the pictures using the words and phrases given.

| Andy feels ____ when he ____. | Jasmin feels ____ when she ____. | Meg feels ____ when she ____. | David feels ____ when someone ____. |

```
        touched                         lie to him
        disappointed                    hear bad news
        shocked                         fail tests
        offended                        read a touching story
```

B. Listen to people talking about what they usually do when they're in certain moods and complete the chart.

	Feelings	Things they do			Feelings	Things they do
1				3		
2				4		

C. With your partner, make up conversations about the feelings listed below. Follow the example. You may use the expressions given below.

- annoyed   • depressed   • nervous   • exhausted

Example

A: You don't look good. Is something wrong with you?

B: I'm very depressed. I can't find a part-time job.

A: I'm sorry to hear that.
   Why don't you do something to make yourself feel better?

B: What should I do? What do you do when you feel depressed?

A: I usually go out for a walk or drive. Try it. It might make you feel better.

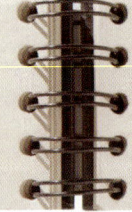

not ready enough for the driving test	hang out with friends	go to a movie
couldn't get enough sleep last night	go shopping / dancing	play sports
saw people littering on the street	try to take it easy	get some sleep
broke up with my boy / girlfriend		chat online

Reading

A. In our lives, embarrassing moments can happen at any time. Below is an article from a magazine where people talk about their most embarrassing moments. Read about how embarrassed they were.

I've never been so embarrassed in my life!

Watch out for the boss!
I was talking about my boss to my co-workers in the hallway. My boss gave me a bunch of reports that were due that week. I told my co-workers how lazy and selfish he is. But then, I was so embarrassed and shocked when I found out that my boss was right behind me. I did my best to explain to him that I was joking. I was upset at my co-workers for not giving me a sign that our boss was standing right behind me!
— Ken, 33, NY

Faking it!
I was playing in a school football league and I was quite a good center fielder. However, I got so embarrassed and awful after I made a fool of myself during one of the games. It was an important match that everyone was wildly excited about. Almost all the students came to watch and cheer. My girlfriend was also there. When I got the ball, I ran and I wanted to look cool. So, I waved at my girlfriend and blew her a kiss. Suddenly, I tripped and fell on my face. I was too embarrassed to stand up, so I just pretended that I had fainted.
— Scott, 18, Pennsylvania

FALLEN SKIRT
One day, all my clothes were in the washing machine, so I wore my mom's skirt. It was a little bit big for me, but I thought it was OK. But then I realized my mistake. I was embarrassed when my skirt fell down on the street. Everybody was looking at me and laughing. I really wanted to crawl under a rock. I quickly pulled up my skirt back up and ran without even looking back.
— Sonya, 16, Las Vegas

B. With your partner, discuss the following questions.

1. Have you had similar experiences to the ones above?
2. Try to remember a moment when you were embarrassed. When was it? What happened?
3. What did you do to try to save face?
4. Try to tell your own story to your partner.
5. Try to tell your partner's story to the class.

Writing

A. In your daily life, things going on around you affect how you feel. What makes you feel good? And what makes you feel bad? Choose one of the topics below and write a short passage about it.

1. Describe the things that make you happy in your daily life.
2. Describe one experience that made you very angry.
3. Describe a moment when you felt depressed.
4. Describe a moment when you get nervous.

Example

I believe happiness does not come from something very special. It comes from small things that you have in your daily life. I take a warm bath after getting home, and I watch soap operas before going to bed. That makes me feel happy and relaxed. When I watch a soap opera, I always put myself into the characters' shoes. I feel so happy when I correctly guess the ending.

05 Have you ever gone bungee jumping?

Lesson Focus

01 Talking about past experiences and events
02 Talking about how long one has been doing a certain activity
03 Talking about the most memorable experience in one's life
04 Using present perfect and present perfect progressive to talk about the activities continuing from the past up to now

UNIT 05 Have you ever gone bungee jumping?

Get started

A Check (✓) if you've ever done the things in the list below.

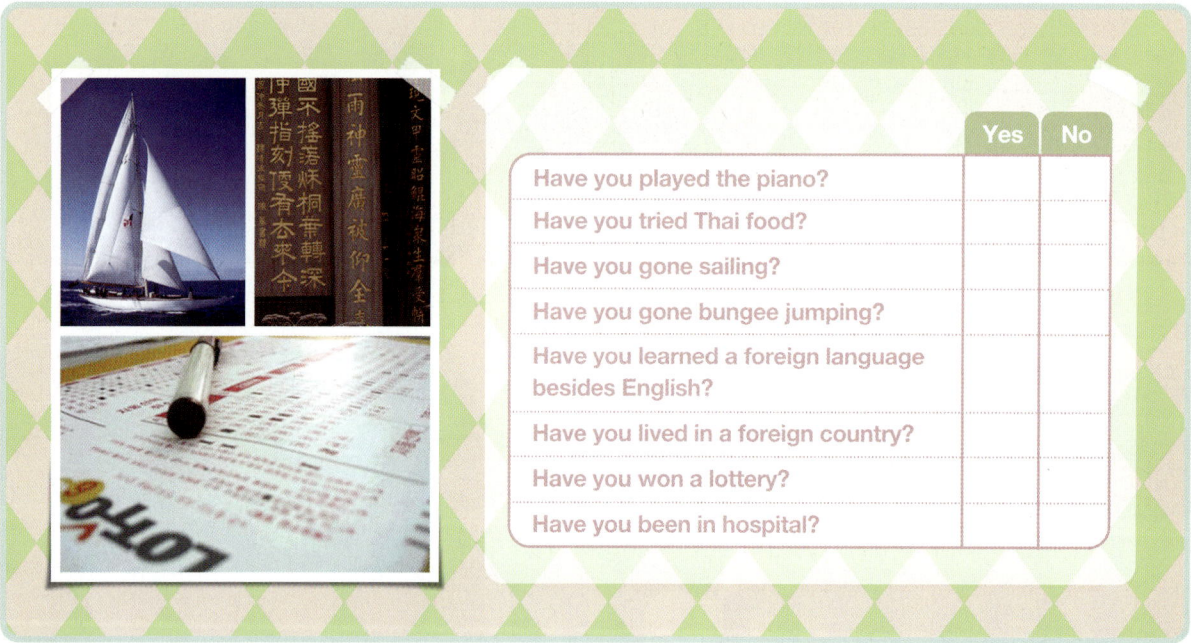

	Yes	No
Have you played the piano?		
Have you tried Thai food?		
Have you gone sailing?		
Have you gone bungee jumping?		
Have you learned a foreign language besides English?		
Have you lived in a foreign country?		
Have you won a lottery?		
Have you been in hospital?		

Discuss these questions with your partner.
1. Which things have you done?
2. Which are the things you haven't done before?
3. Which was the best experience?
4. Which have you done until now?

B. Which of the following have you been doing for a long time? Check (✓) those things. Then write down how long you have been doing them.

	Yes	How long…?
Have you been studying English(or a foreign language) for long?	✓	for seven years / since 2000
Have you been wearing glasses/contact lenses for long?		
Have you been working out for long?		
Have you been working for your company many years?		
Have you been seeing your boy/girlfriend for long?		
Have you been using your cell phone for long?		

Talk together 🎧

Listen to the dialogue and practice.

Ryan: Long time no see. What have you been up to?
Marilyn: I've just come back from a business trip to Japan.
Ryan: Oh, how long have you been away?
Marilyn: I've been away for nearly three weeks. By the way, have you been to Japan?
Ryan: Yes, I've been there twice.
Marilyn: Then have you ever visited one of the hot springs in the mountains?
Ryan: Of course. Many tourists go to Japan for it. What about you?
Marilyn: Yes, I have. It was an amazing experience. I'd like to visit Japan again.
Ryan: And have you gone skiing? There are many good ski resorts worth visiting in winter.
Marilyn: No, I haven't. I couldn't make time to go skiing, but I've tried many different kinds of sushi. All of them were delicious.

Language focus

What have you been up to?	I've just come back from a business trip.
Have you been to Japan?	Yes, I have been there twice. No, I haven't. / I've never been there.
How long have you been away?	I've been away for about three weeks.
Have you ever gone skiing?	Yes, I have. / No, I haven't.
How long have you been learning English?	I have been learning English for six years. 　　　　　　　　　　　since last year. 　　　　　　　　　　　since I was in college.

Practice more

A. Make questions using the phrases given in the chart and proper past participle forms of the verbs. Ask your partner the questions and fill in the chart with your partner's responses.

Have you ever...?	Yes	No	If yes,	
Be on TV			When was that?	
Meet a celebrity			Who was that?	
Have a pet			What did you have?	
Meet your true love			Who was that?	
Fly in a helicopter			When was that?	

B. Work with your partner. Practice the dialogues using the words given.

A: Have you traveled a lot?
B: Yes, I have.
A: Really? Have you ever been to China?
B: Yes, I've been to China twice. How about you? Have you been to China?
A: No, I haven't, but I've been to India.

- play in a band - play the guitar - play the synthesizer
- drive a car - drive a van - drive a truck
- run a marathon - run for 10 km - run a half course
- go to see a ballet - go many times - go to see a modern dance

A: Have you been studying Chinese for long?
B: Yes, I have.
A: How long have you been studying it?
B: I've been studying it for two years / since 2005.

• do weight training	• for one month
• see your boy / girlfriend	• since last year
• play the piano	• since 2004
• write poems	• for two years
• play tennis	• since I was twenty

42 • UNIT 05

Let's do it 1

A. What kind of sports have you played? What kind of food have you tried? And what countries have you visited? Check the items you've done.

Have you ever…?

gone rafting
in-line skating
snorkeling
snowboarding
horseback riding
hang-gliding

tried Mexican food
Thai food
Indian food
Turkish food
French food
Greek food

been to Europe
Africa
China
America
Russia
a tropical island

B. Listen to people talking about their experiences and complete the sentences below by filling in the blanks.

1	Nick has _____ three times.
	Michelle _____, but she has _____, and rock climbing.
2	Ken has _____ food.
	Helen _____, but she has _____, and Cuban food.
3	Bill _____ Bali.
	Megan _____, and Greece.

C. With your partner, talk about the experiences you've had with sports, food, and travel. You may use the expressions in Part **A** and the listening scripts in Part **B**.

Example

A: Have you ever gone rafting?
B: Yes, I have.
A: How many times have you done that?
B: I've done that every summer for five years.
A: When did you do that for the first time?
B: Five years ago when I was in college. How about you? Have you gone rafting?
A: No, I haven't. But I'd like to try it sometime.

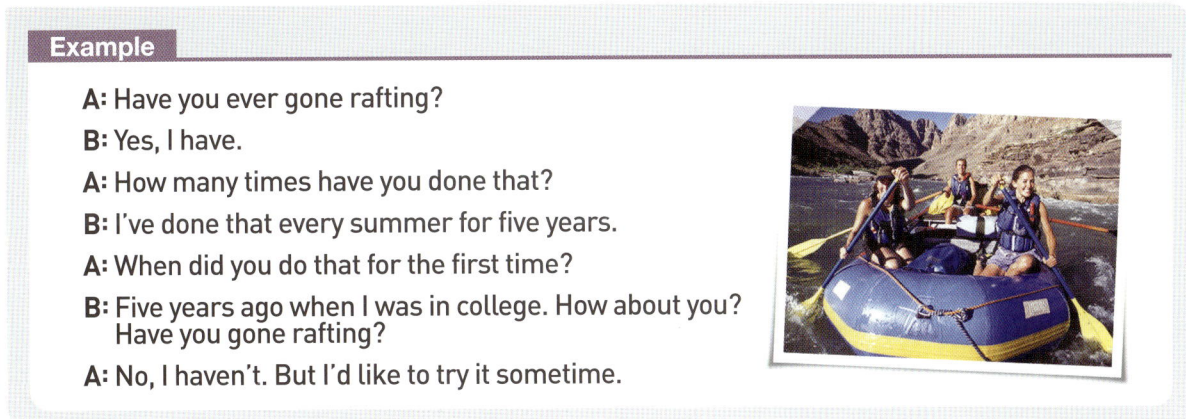

Let's do it 2

A. What kinds of activities have you been doing for a long period of time? Choose some of the activities and write sentences about how long you have been doing them. You may use the words below.

- play sports (run marathons / play ping pong / go hiking / go cycling / do yoga...)
- learn to cook / bake
- grow plants
- take care of pets
- study foreign languages
- work as a volunteer / part-timer

Example

I've been doing yoga since last year.
I've been studying Chinese for two years.
I've been taking care of cats since I was 20.

B. Listen to three interview clips. After listening, check (✓) if each of the following statements is true or false. If the statement is false, correct it.

Conversation		True	False
1	Jennifer has been going out with a rock musician.		
	She has been with him for 19 months.		
2	Mr. Dickson has been working for the company more than 20 years.		
	Mr. Dickson has won the 'Employee of the Year' award three times.		
3	Susan has been doing aerobics and going hiking.		
	She has been on diets many times.		

C. Work with your partner. Interview each other about one thing you've been doing successfully. It could be anything you've been doing in your everyday life. You may use the sentences in Part **A** and the listening scripts in Part **B**.

Example

A: Have you been doing anything special?
B: I've been working as a volunteer.
A: How long have you been doing that?
B: I've been doing that for three years.
A: Why have you done that for so long?
B: It's really worth doing. I can help people in need.

Reading

A. These people are telling about a great experience in their lives in the reader's column of a magazine.

The one great thing I've done so far…

I think the best thing I have ever done is visit many countries. I've been to countries in Europe such as England, France, Italy, and Spain. I've also been to Turkey, Australia, China, Japan as well as the U.S. While traveling, I've met many good people, tried a variety of foods, and visited interesting places. Above all, the best part of my travels was the friends I made. I've been keeping in touch with most of them. Through my experiences, I've been able to better understand the world and people from various ethnic and cultural backgrounds. Traveling has brought me many opportunities, so my journeys will go on as long as I'm alive.

My name is Markus and I am from Switzerland. I've climbed mountains since I was twenty. I've climbed Mt. Everest, Mt. Kilimangaro, and the Mont Blanc Range. In addition, I've taken part in 18 expeditions. Since I started climbing mountains, I've met great climbers. Michelle is an American climber, and she's been climbing for 18 years. It can be dangerous to climb mountains like Mt. Everest. I've suffered from frostbite several times. But, every time I reach a peak, I am moved by the beauty of the world and nature. That's why I've been enjoying climbing up mountains. They're always there waiting for me!

B. With your partner, discuss the following questions.

1. Have you traveled to foreign countries? Where have you been?

2. If you have a chance to travel around the world, where would you like to go? What would you like to do while traveling?

3. Have you ever gone mountain climbing? If yes, where have you gone climbing? If no, would you like to go climbing someday? To where?

4. What do you think is the best thing you've ever done in your life?

Writing

A. You've probably done various kinds of things to make your life better. Think of one thing you've started this year and have been doing up to now. Write about it briefly. You may use one of the activities listed below.

- be on a diet for …
- work as a volunteer since …
- read more than five books a month since …
- take an English (or other languages) course for …
- learn to cook / dance for …
- work out at the gym since …

Example

I've been working as a volunteer since January. It's really worth doing. I have visited a nursing home for disabled people. I've done chores like cooking, cleaning, and giving baths. Through the volunteer work, I was able to understand disabled people better, so I have thought how I can help them better. It's a great experience to help people in need.

06 What's the purpose of your trip?

Lesson Focus

- 01 Reserving a flight and going through immigration
- 02 Reserving a hotel room and asking for hotel services
- 03 Talking about travel plans and itineraries
- 04 Talking about types of trips and vacation activities
- 05 Writing emails about one's travels

UNIT 06 What's the purpose of your trip?

Get started

A. There are various types of trips a person can take. If you'd like to go on trips to other countries, what types of trips would you like to take? Where would you like to go? Check (✓) the types of trips and places.

Types of trips	
go camping	go backpacking
go trekking	go to a resort
go sightseeing	go cruising
go shopping	go skiing

Destinations	
Mediterranean	South East Asia
Eastern Europe	South America
Africa	Australia / Oceania
tropical islands	Middle East
Other:	

Discuss these questions with your partner.

1. What types of trips do you like to take? Why?
2. What are the places you'd like to visit most? Why would you like to visit those places?
3. Do you travel a lot? Where do you usually go? How do you get there?
   What do you usually do there? Where do you stay?

B. When you travel to remote places or foreign countries, you usually use airports and hotels. Choose the right words for the items in the pictures.

Airport

Hotel

❶ toiletries　　❷ check-in counter　　❸ housekeeper　　❹ security check
❺ baggage claim　　❻ reception　　❼ gate　　❽ bellhop

Talk together 🎧

Listen to the dialogue and practice.

Kevin:	Are you still planning to go trekking in Nepal during the next vacation?
Meg:	Definitely, that's been one of my lifelong dreams.
Kevin:	So, are you going by yourself or taking a package tour?
Meg:	I'm going with two members of my hiking club.
Kevin:	Then did you make all the reservations for the flight, hotels and so on?
Meg:	Sure. We got lucky with plane tickets at specially discounted prices, and we booked rooms at a decent hotel with reasonable rates.
Kevin:	That's good! So, when are you leaving?
Meg:	I'm leaving on August 3rd.
Kevin:	Sounds like you're all set. How long will you be staying there?
Meg:	For ten days. We're going sightseeing in Kathmandu and trekking around the Himalayas.
Kevin:	Wow, sounds fabulous!

Language focus

Reserving a flight

North Eastern Airlines. May I help you?	I'd like to make a reservation for two seats to New York.
	I'd like a round-trip ticket from LA to Miami.
When do you want to leave?	I want to leave early on Monday, the 31st.
What date would you like to fly?	I'd like to fly on Tuesday, the 7th.

At immigration

What is the purpose of your trip / visit to America?	I'm here on business / vacation.
	I'm here to visit my relatives / friends.
	to attend a language school / conference.
How long do you plan to stay?	I'll be here for about two weeks.
How long will you be staying here?	I'll be here until I finish my studies.

At hotels

What can I do for you? / How may I help you?	I'd like to book a single room / double room / suite.
How long will you be staying?	For two nights, from May 12th to 14th.
What are your rates?	The single room is $100 a day.

What's the purpose of your trip? • 49

Practice more

A. Here are some telephone notes about flight reservations. With your partner, practice making dialogues like the example below. Use the expressions in the Language focus section.

1. → Beijing
early in the morning
Wed 5th
7am

2. Korea ↔ LA
late in the evening
Wed 13th
9:45pm

3. → Florida
morning
September 15th
10:15am

4. Korea ↔ Sydney
in the afternoon
Sat 19th
only 8:45pm

Example

A: North Eastern Airlines. What can I do for you?
B: I'd like a one-way ticket to Boston, please.
A: When do you want to leave? (What date would you like to fly?)
B: I want to leave (I'd like to fly) early in the morning on Tuesday the 8th.
A: OK, there's a flight at 6:30 am. Is that fine with you?   B: Great.
A: May I have your name and phone number?   B: Tim Barron. 673-3556.

B. With your partner, practice making dialogues about reserving hotel rooms. Try to use the expressions given and your own words.

Example

A: Travel Inn, how can I help you?
B: I'd like to make a reservation for a room.
A: How long will you be staying?
B: For three nights, March 15th to 18th.
A: What kind of room would you like?
B: I'd like a single room. What's the rate?
A: The singleroom is $100 per night.
B: OK. I'll take it.
A: Good. May I have your name and phone number?

- How long would you like to stay here?
- A double room
- How much is the room per night?

C. When you travel to foreign countries, you have to talk with an immigration officer at the airport. Practice the dialogue below. Use the expressions given or those in Language focus.

A: Welcome to Paris. May I see your passport?   B: Here you are.
A: What is the purpose of your trip?   B: I'm here to visit a friend of mine.
A: How long do you plan to stay? (How long will you be staying here?)
B: I plan to stay (I'll be staying) here for about two weeks.

- to travel / backpack
- to attend a(n) conference / seminar / exhibition
- to take a language course / study at graduate school

Let's do it 1

A. When you stay in a hotel, you may require some of the hotel's services and facilities. Match the pictures and proper phrases below.

- room service
- wake-up call
- a room with a lake view
- heating problems

B. Listen to four phone conversations between guests and hotel staff. Then fill in the table below.

Conversation	The customer asks for
1	
2	
3	
4	

C. With your partner, make up dialogues about typical requests at a hotel using the words below. Refer to the listening scripts in Part **B** and try to be creative.

- a room with an ocean / a mountain / a lake view
- room / cleaning service
- Internet access
- wake-up call
- tour service
- airport shuttle service

Example

A: Hello. What can I do for you?
B: Can I get a wake-up call?
A: Of course. When do you need it?
B: I need to wake up at 6 am.
A: OK, we'll give you a wake-up call tomorrow morning at 6.

What's the purpose of your trip? • 51

Let's do it 2

A. A lot of people hope to go on a trip to a tropical island for vacation. If you could spend your vacation on one of the following islands, which island would you choose?

- Bali   • Maldives   • Fiji   • Hawaii   • Saipan   • Cebu

Why would you like to go there? Check (✓) all the things you'd like to do.

getting a suntan ☐	going scuba diving ☐	taking tours ☐
sailing a yacht ☐	going paragliding ☐	taking a cruise ☐
going to a folk dancing show ☐	going sea walking ☐	going white-water rafting ☐

B. A couple, who are going to get married soon, plan to spend five days and four nights in Bali for their honeymoon. Listen to their conversation and complete their itinerary.

Day 1
Day 2
Day 3
Day 4
Day 5

C. Work with your partner. Pretend you're going on a vacation to Cebu or Fiji. Talk about where you're going to stay and what you are going to do by using the itineraries below. Follow the listening script in Part **B**.

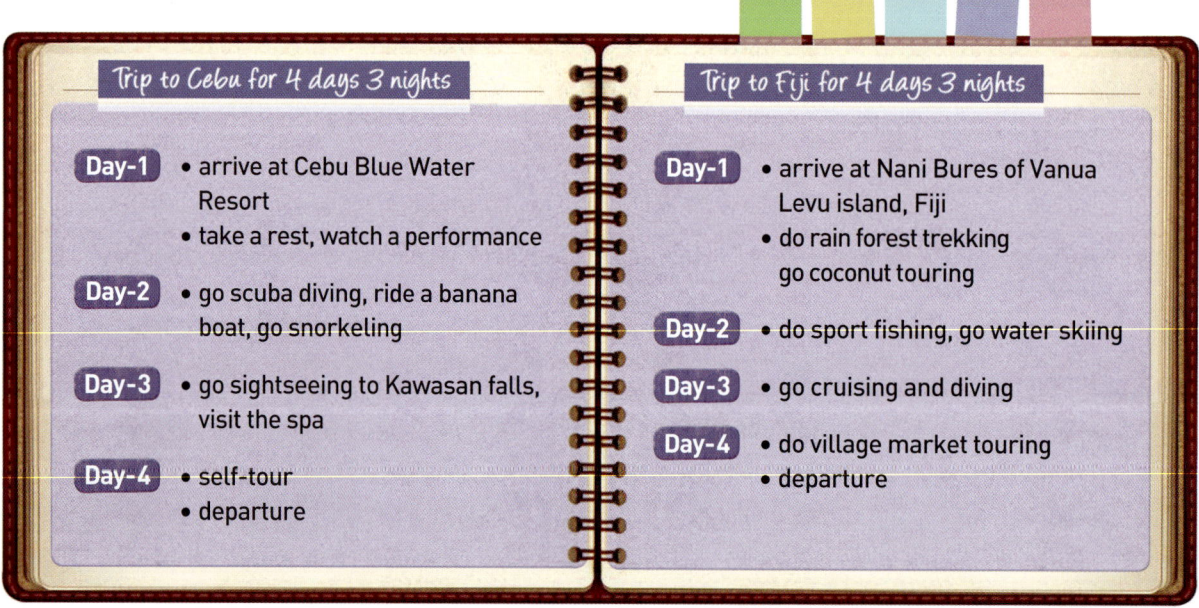

Trip to Cebu for 4 days 3 nights

- Day-1
  • arrive at Cebu Blue Water Resort
  • take a rest, watch a performance
- Day-2
  • go scuba diving, ride a banana boat, go snorkeling
- Day-3
  • go sightseeing to Kawasan falls, visit the spa
- Day-4
  • self-tour
  • departure

Trip to Fiji for 4 days 3 nights

- Day-1
  • arrive at Nani Bures of Vanua Levu island, Fiji
  • do rain forest trekking
    go coconut touring
- Day-2
  • do sport fishing, go water skiing
- Day-3
  • go cruising and diving
- Day-4
  • do village market touring
  • departure

Reading

A. Below is one of the articles from a newly published travel magazine, 'Leisure Life.' Read the following article.

Top 3 Recommended Tourist Sites of the Year

Maldives-Beach Paradise

Do you love the ocean? Here you can relax, swim, sunbathe, get massages and enjoy the local cuisine! You can find good places to shop anywhere as well. Whether you stay at a resort or in a hotel, you can find a traditional local market nearby. Sun, sand, ocean, underwater coral gardens,... It is a perfect natural combination for the ideal tropical holiday destination. Also, you can dance on the beach at night under the stars. It's perfect for romance, too!

Wild Safari in Southern Africa

If you love nature, this is the vacation for you! You can take photos of wild animals. You can see beautiful mountains and lakes. For adventure seekers, we have a special program, the Beaten Path. This program has several physical activities. For example, you might climb Mt. Kilimanjaro or take part in a gorilla trek in Uganda. This long walking through safari takes you to the most dramatic, scenic, and wild areas of Southern Africa.

Snow White Hokkaido

For ski lovers in winter! Ski on some of the most beautiful mountains in Asia. Skiing in Japan can be expensive, but, if you stay at a Minshuku, a private guesthouse, it is cheaper. There are many Minshukus located throughout the ski resort. Enjoy fresh air, exercise and great views in the heart of Japan.

B. Discuss these questions with your partner.

1. Among the three tourist sites, where would you like to go the most? Why?
2. Do you have a vacation plan in mind? Where are you going and what are you going to do?
3. What were the best tourist sites you have ever been to?
4. Which tourist sites in your country would you recommend to visitors / tourists / foreigners? Share your recommendations with your classmates.

Writing

A. This is an e-mail from your imaginary friend, Andy. Read his e-mail, then write a reply by imagining that you are on vacation in Korea.

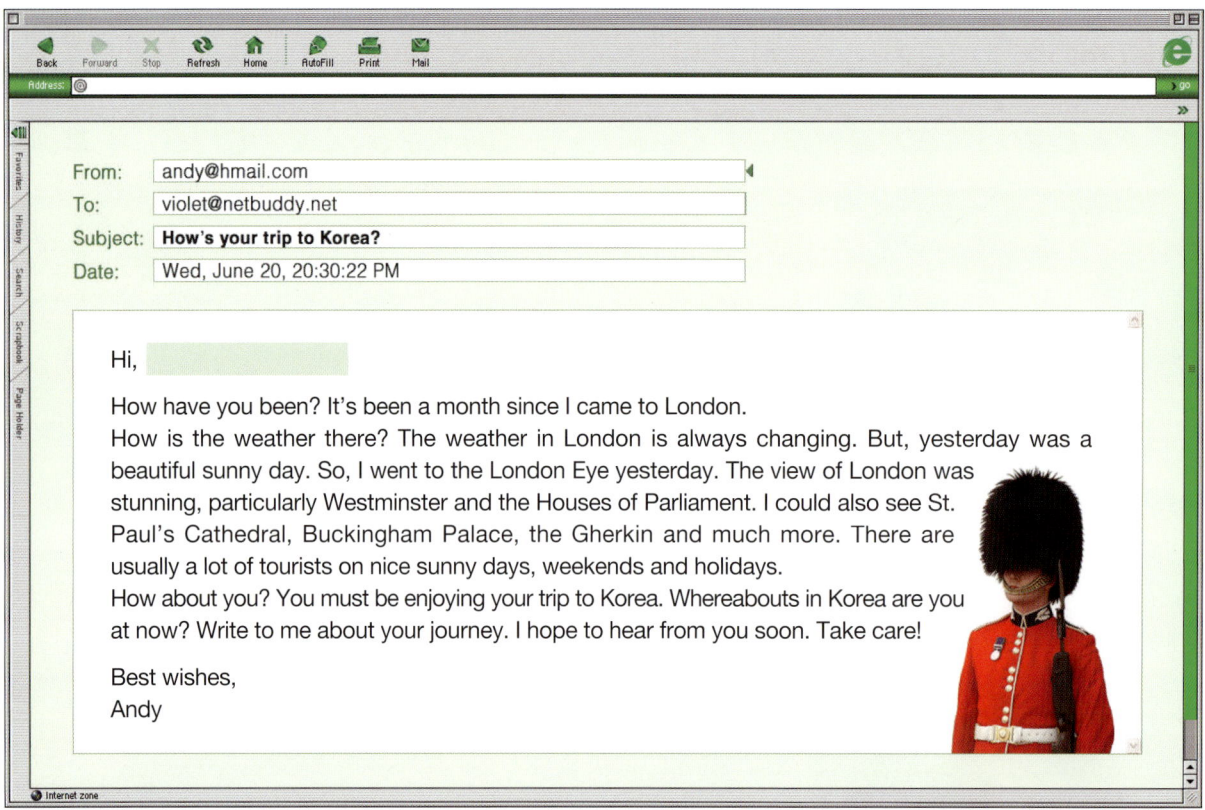

From: andy@hmail.com
To: violet@netbuddy.net
Subject: How's your trip to Korea?
Date: Wed, June 20, 20:30:22 PM

Hi,

How have you been? It's been a month since I came to London.
How is the weather there? The weather in London is always changing. But, yesterday was a beautiful sunny day. So, I went to the London Eye yesterday. The view of London was stunning, particularly Westminster and the Houses of Parliament. I could also see St. Paul's Cathedral, Buckingham Palace, the Gherkin and much more. There are usually a lot of tourists on nice sunny days, weekends and holidays.
How about you? You must be enjoying your trip to Korea. Whereabouts in Korea are you at now? Write to me about your journey. I hope to hear from you soon. Take care!

Best wishes,
Andy

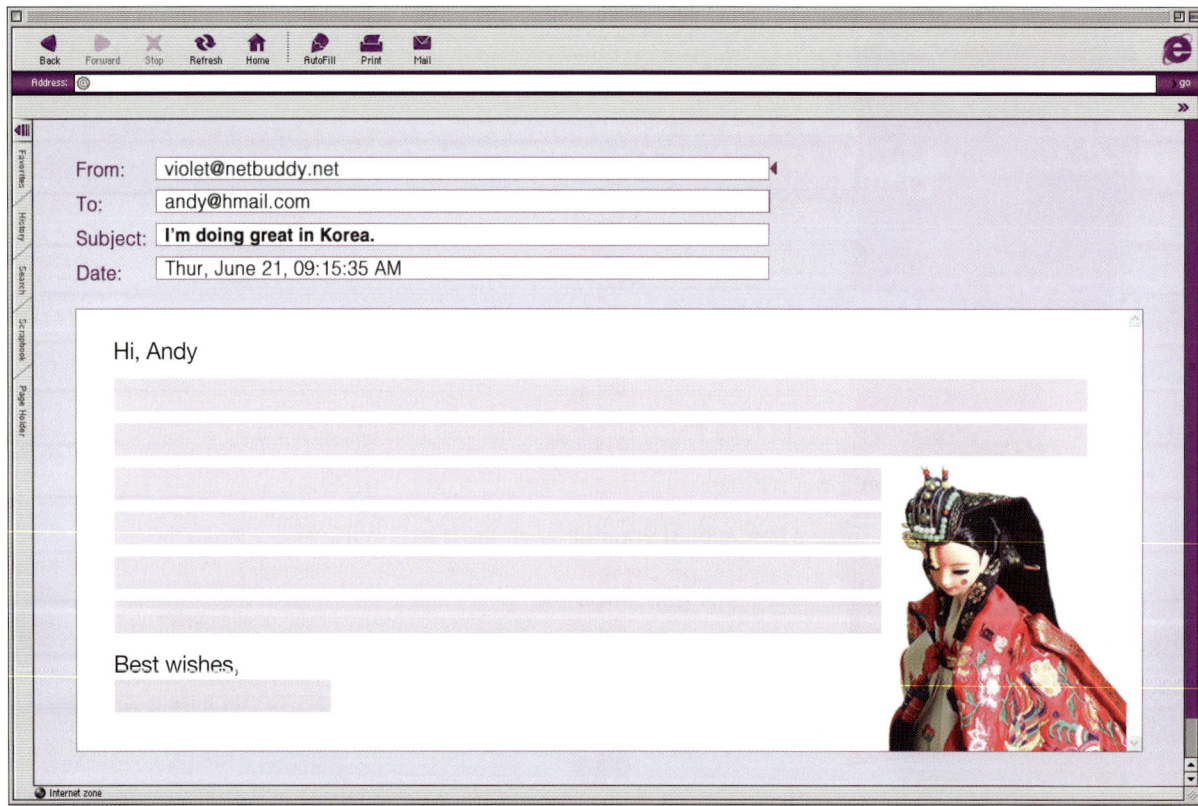

From: violet@netbuddy.net
To: andy@hmail.com
Subject: I'm doing great in Korea.
Date: Thur, June 21, 09:15:35 AM

Hi, Andy

Best wishes,

07 Could you get me some water?

Lesson Focus

01 Making requests and accepting or refusing requests
02 Asking for permission and giving and declining permission
03 Giving reasons for declining requests and permission
04 Using *Can, Would you mind*...to make requests and ask for permission

Could you get me some water?

Get started

A. What are these people requesting? Complete their requests using the words from the list.

- turning down
- give... a hand
- keep... open
- answer

B. What permission are these people asking for? Complete their questions using the words form the list.

- Would you mind
- May
- Is it OK

Talk together

Listen to the dialogue and practice.

June: Hi, Kelly. How is studying for the psychology exam going?
Kelly: I haven't done much. Actually, I lack time to finish reading all the chapters before the exam. Do you happen to have summary notes?
June: Well, you are lucky. I have them.
Kelly: That's great. Would you mind lending them to me?
June: No problem, but they're a bit messy to read.
Kelly: That's alright. Could you get the notes now so I can photocopy them?
June: Oh, I'm sorry, I can't right now. The notes are in my dorm room, and I have the study group meeting now. Is it OK if I give them to you after the meeting?
Kelly: No problem. I'll be in the library, so call me when you're done with the meeting.
June: OK. See you then.

Language focus

Making Requests	Accepting / Refusing Requests
Could (Would, Can) you answer the phone?	Yes, of course. / No problem. / OK. Sure, I'd be glad to. I'm sorry, I can't right now. I'm sorry, but I'm busy now.
Would (Do) you mind opening the door?	Sure. / No problem. / All right. Yes. I'm afraid I do. I'm sorry, but my hands are full.
Could you give my dictionary back? I need it now.	I'm sorry, I forgot it. It's in my locker, I'll get you it now.

Asking for Permission	Giving / Refusing Permission
Could (May, Can) I park here?	Sure. / Certainly. / Of course. / OK.
Would it be possible (for me) to park here?	I'm sorry, but parking is not allowed here. Sorry, I am afraid you are not allowed.
Would you mind if I use this pen?	No, of course not. / No, go ahead. / Not at all. I am sorry, but it's out of ink.
Is it OK if I use your dictionary?	Sure, go ahead.

Practice more

A. With your partner, take turns making requests and responding to them using the information given below.

> **Example**
>
> very busy this week / help me with this report
> 😞 busy with the presentation
>
> A: I am very busy this week. Could you help me? (Would you mind helping me) with this report?
>
> B: I'm sorry, but I'm busy with the presentation.

😊😊😊😊😊😊😊😊😊😊	😞😞😞😞😞😞😞😞😞😞
have a cast on my leg carry these boxes	have a phone call / turn the volume down volume button is not functioning
forget to bring my textbook share yours with me	miss the class yesterday / lend me your notes already lent mine to someone else
feel very sick get me some medicine	noisy outside / close the door stuffy and hot in here

B. Match the phrases on the left with the related expressions on the right. Then with your partner, take turns asking for permission and responding it. Follow the example.

have a dog at home	as long as you switch it to vibration mode
try these clothes on	allergic to dogs
drink coffee during the performance	may try on as many as you like
take a look at this document	no eating and drinking is allowed
keep my mobile phone on during the meeting? I am expecting a phone call	welcome to take a look at it

> **Example**
>
> A: May I (Would you mind if I) (Would it be possible for me to) have a dog at home?
>
> B: Sorry, I am afraid you are not allowed. I am allergic to dogs.

Let's do it 1

A. Some office workers are busy with their works in the picture. They are making requests to their co-workers. Complete the words they are saying using the expressions from the list.

- go get this document bound
- send someone to take a look at the copier
- make ten copies of this report
- call a courier service and send this package

B. Listen to the conversations and fill in the chart. Write reasons if the request is refused.

Conversation	Accepted ◎ / Refused ✗	Reason
1		
2		
3		
4		

C. With your partner, make dialogues using the expressions from Part **A**. Use the scripts of the conversations in Part **B** and the example below.

> **Example**
>
> A: My hands are full. Would you mind making ten copies of this material?
> B: Of course not, but the photocopier is not working right now.
> A: Then could you call someone to fix it?
> B: Certainly.

Let's do it 2

A-①. Peter, who is a college student, has been talking to the people below to ask for permission. Listen to the conversations and number the pictures.

A-②. Listen again and fill in the chart. Write the reasons if permission is refused.

Conversation	Given ◯ / Refused ✕	Reasons for refusing
1		
2		
3		
4		

B. Work with a partner. Make dialogues about asking for permission using the situations below. Follow the example and try to use your own creativity.

❶ You forget to bring your laptop, but your friend has one now.
❷ You can't find anywhere to park your car. You find one spot, which is reserved for disabled people only.
❸ You want to invite your friends over to your dorm room. Before you invite your friends over, you need to ask your roommate for permission.
❹ You belong to a basketball team. Your team wants to practice until late in the gym. You need to ask the guard to leave it open until late.

> **Example**
>
> A: Oh, no! I forgot to bring my laptop today. I think I left it at home. Is it OK for me to use your laptop for a moment?
>
> B: Sure, but not for a long time. I need it for my presentation.

Reading

A. People have a chance to finally say what they really want to say in this magazine article. See their hidden problems and requests.

wanna talk! talk! talk!

We sometimes face situations where we cannot freely say what we want to say. We keep it to ourselves and end up getting sick. This survey was done with 50 youngsters aged 15~25, asking them what they really want to say, but they can't. Let's look at the top ten issues that people have difficulties speaking out about.

TOP 01 | Roomate problem (38%)

I have lived in the school dormitory with my roommate for a year. I am an early bird type of person, but my roommate is a night owl. She is always on the phone with her boyfriend and loves listening to loud music, even late at night. It's killing me because I tend to go to bed before 12. One day, I was especially annoyed by the loud heavy metal music that my roomie was listening to because I had an exam the next day. But, I still could not tell her to turn the volume down. So, here I am talking to you, Roommate! Could you stop talking to your boyfriend on the phone all night and turn down the music?

- Anna, 19

TOP 02 | Boyfriend's issue (25%)

My mom somehow doesn't like my boyfriend, and doesn't want me to hang out with him. It could be because my boyfriend is four years younger than me. She always scolds me for being late and for going on many dates with him. However, I could tell her that my boyfriend is such a caring and thoughtful person even though he is younger than me. He cares about me a lot and he is the sweetest person I've ever seen. I hope my mom starts to like him, as well. Mom, could you please let me go out with my young boyfriend? I will promise to keep my curfew from now on.

- Julie, 20

TOP 03

B. Discuss the following questions with your partner.

1. If you have something you'd like to make a complaint about to someone, what is your complaint?
2. Have you ever been in the same shoes as the person in Top 01? If yes, describe the situation.
3. Have you ever been in the same shoes as the person in Top 02? If yes, describe the situation.
4. Do you have something to ask someone permission for?
5. Do you have something that you want to speak out about, but can't let it out?
What is that you want to speak out about?

Writing

A. Pretend that you are facing the situation below. Write a letter to whom it may concern. An example is given to help you with your letter.

Example

Situation You work part-time in a convenience store.
You work six hours a day, three days a week.
You did not get this month's paycheck.
You need to pay your rent by the end of this week.
You want to write a letter to your boss about the payment.

Dear Mr. Anderson,

I believe this is hard to talk about, so here I am writing this letter to you. As you know, I work here as a part-timer for six hours a day, three days a week. That is a total of 72 hours a month. However, I still have not received my paycheck for this month. Would you mind considering that I need to pay my rent by the end of this week? So, would it be possible to collect my pay before this Thursday? That would be much thankful.

Sincerely yours,
Crystal

Situation You are an office worker.
You've worked for two years at this office.
You need a break.
You are planning to go on a trip to Hawaii for seven days.
You want to write a letter to your boss to ask for time off.

Dear

08 While you are on vacation, what will you do?

Lesson Focus

01 Talking about favorite free time activities and future plans
02 Talking about activities one will do in a certain situation in the future
03 Making invitations and accepting and refusing invitations
04 Using time clauses with *when, if, while, before, after* to talk about future plans
05 Using *Would you like to...* to make invitations

UNIT 08 While you are on vacation, what will you do?

Get started

A. What do you enjoy doing when you have free time? Put the activities you like to do in the correct category. You may use the expressions from the box below or your own words.

Entertainment	Outdoor activities / Sports	Others

- go to the movies
- play extreme sports
- go dancing
- have parties
- go trekking
- go to plays
- go to concerts
- go shopping
- go to exhibitions
- go on trips
- play musical instruments
- take photos

Talk about the following questions with your partner.

1. Which do you prefer? Spending your free time by yourself or with someone?
2. If you like to spend your free time alone, what do you enjoy doing?
3. If you like to spend your free time with someone, what do you do together?
4. Do you sometimes invite someone to do the above activities together? Who do you usually invite?

B. What will you do if you find yourself in the following situations? Choose the appropriate expressions from the list below or Part **A** to complete the sentences.

While I'm on vacation, I will get plenty of rest.
When the weather is very mild and sunny, _____
If I have more free time, _____
After I finish work / school, _____
Before I go to bed, _____
As soon as I get home, _____

- get plenty of rest
- go for a drive
- blog
- do exercises
- watch a movie
- get more sleep
- learn new things
- do household chores

Talk together

Listen to the dialogue and practice.

Morris: What do you like to do when you have free time?

Olivia: I like to go to all kinds of performances like musicals, plays, and dances. I went to see the musical 'Chicago' last Sunday.

Morris: Sounds exciting. I don't have much free time.

Olivia: That's a shame. So if you have more free time, what will you do?

Morris: I'll go hang-gliding in the summer and skiing in the winter.

Olivia: Oh, I'd like to go hang-gliding someday. I hope you can get more free time and do those activities. By the way, I'm having a housewarming party this Friday. Would you like to come?

Morris: I'd like to, but I have to work the night shift that day.

Olivia: Sorry to hear that. Anyway, how about going hang-gliding together when you're free?

Morris: Good idea. I'll let you know when I have time for it.

Language focus

Time clauses

When you go on vacation, what will you do?	**When** I go on vacation, I'll go sightseeing.
If you're on vacation, what will you do?	**If** I'm on vacation, I'll take day trips around the island.
While you are in Bali, what will you do?	**While** I am in Bali, I'll go swimming every day.
Before you go on vacation, what will you do?	**Before** I go on vacation, I'll finish painting the house.
After you visit Bali, what will you do?	**After** I visit Bali, I'll go to Hong Kong.
As soon as you arrive in Bali, what will you do?	**As soon as** I arrive in Bali, I'll get some rest.

Making invitations

How / what about going to a concert this Friday?
Would you like to go to a concert this Friday?
Why don't we go to a concert this Friday?
Let's go to a concert this Friday.

Accepting

Yes, I'd like to / I'd love to.
Sure, that's a good idea. / That sounds great.

Refusing

Oh, I'm sorry. I can't. I'm busy that night.
I'd love to, but I can't. I have to study.
I'd like to, but I'm doing something else.

Practice more

A. Fill in the chart below. First fill in the blanks with your own answers or the expressions given. Then take turns interviewing each other. Follow the example.

...what will you do?	You	Your partner
If you take a week off,		
After you finish work/school,		
When you have free time,		
While you're on vacation,		

- watch movies / DVDs
- go swimming / bowling / cycling...
- play soccer / tennis...
- read books / comic books
- go to exhibitions / concerts...
- go on a trip / travel to...
- take up a hobby
- catch up on some sleep
- visit hometown / friends...

Example

A: If you take a week off, what will you do?

B: I'll travel to China if I take a week off. A friend of mine works there, so I really want to visit him. How about you?

A: If I take a week off, I'll read comic books and get some rest.

B: Those sound like good ideas, too.

B. Take turns with your partner suggesting things to do this weekend and responding to them. If you refuse any of the suggestions or invitations, be sure to give reasons. You may use the expressions below.

If you are free this Saturday, would you like to go to a concert with me?

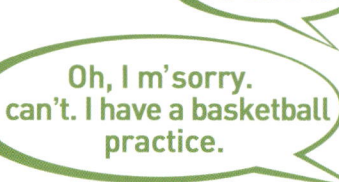
Yes, I'd love to.

Oh, I'm sorry. I can't. I have a basketball practice.

Invitations	Reasons for Refusing
go to the ballet performance	finish all my reports by this weekend
go to a barbecue	go see the doctor
go to a jazz club/ hip-hop club	go to a family gathering
play baseball / soccer	take care of my younger brother
go skiing / in-line skating	meet my friends
watch a K-1 match	attend a workshop

Let's do it 1

A. Make four questions on your own using the time adverbs and phrases given. Then with your partner, take turns asking and answering the questions. Write down the answers in the blanks.

If	be done with the final exams
When / While	get off from work
After / Before	take a week off
As soon as	be in Las Vegas (or some place else)

❶ _____, what will you do? → _____

❷ _____, what will you do? → _____

❸ _____, what will you do? → _____

❹ _____, what will you do? → _____

B. Listen to people talking about their plans and complete the sentences below.

Conversation	They will do...
1	If Cathy gets a week off, she'll take a scuba diving lesson. If Denise _____
2	While Kelly is in Hong Kong, _____ While Amanda _____
3	After Melissa gets off from work, _____ After Jim _____

C. With your partner, make up conversations like the example below. Refer to the listening scripts in Part **B**. Try to use as many different expressions as you can and be creative.

Example

A: If you take a week off, what will you do?

B: If I take a week off, I will go to New Zealand. When(While) I am in New Zealand, I will visit Lord of the Rings filming locations and experience the Mauri culture. How about you? What will you do if you have a week off?

A: I will practice driving. After I practice driving, I'll take the driving test.

Let's do it 2

A. You've found some information about things to do in June on the college bulletin board. Looking at the information with your partner, ask him / her if he / she'd like to do the activities.

Let's Learn Magic!
Two-hour session on how to do magic tricks will be held for you with 100% free of charge
- **When:** 1~3 pm, June 5th, Tue
- **Where:** Main Theater
- **Things to bring:** cards

Graduation Exhibition- Modern Sculpture
The Department of Art and Design student exhibition will be open to students and public. Admission is free!
- **Place:** Rose hall
- **Date:** June 18th ~ 22nd
- **Open hours:** 10 am ~ 4 pm

Yo! Feel the Hip-Hop Beat!
Hip-hop teams have gathered to perform our dance! Come and feel the beat! A dance party offering snacks will be held after the performance.
- **When:** 7:30 pm, June 22nd, Fri
- **Where:** Franklin Auditorium
- **Entrance fee:** $5

Cycling Tour
Cycling is a fun and challenging exercise that keeps you healthy. Sign up for the two-day cycling tour to Lake Tahoe!
- **When:** June 13th ~14th
- **Fee:** $100 (meals & accomodation included)

B. Listen to the conversations and check (✓) if the invitation was accepted or refused. If the invitation was refused, write down the reasons.

Conversation	Accepted ◎ / Refused ✗	Reasons
1		
2		
3		
4		

C. With your partner, practice inviting each other to take part in some activities. You may either accept or politely refuse the invitations by giving appropriate reasons. Be creative.

Accepting

A: Would you like to go out for a coffee after work? I know a great espresso place.
B: Sure, I'd be happy to go.
A: Great! Then I'll see you around seven in front of your office.
B: OK. See you then.

Refusing

A: How about going to a symphony this Friday night? I got two free tickets.
B: Oh, I'd love to, but I can't. I have a family gathering this Friday.
A: Oh, I see. Well... I guess I'll have to find someone else, then.
B: I'm sorry. Maybe next time!

Reading

A. Many people hope to take some time off from their jobs or schools. How about you? The following shows what people say about taking time off on the opinion board of an Internet portal site.

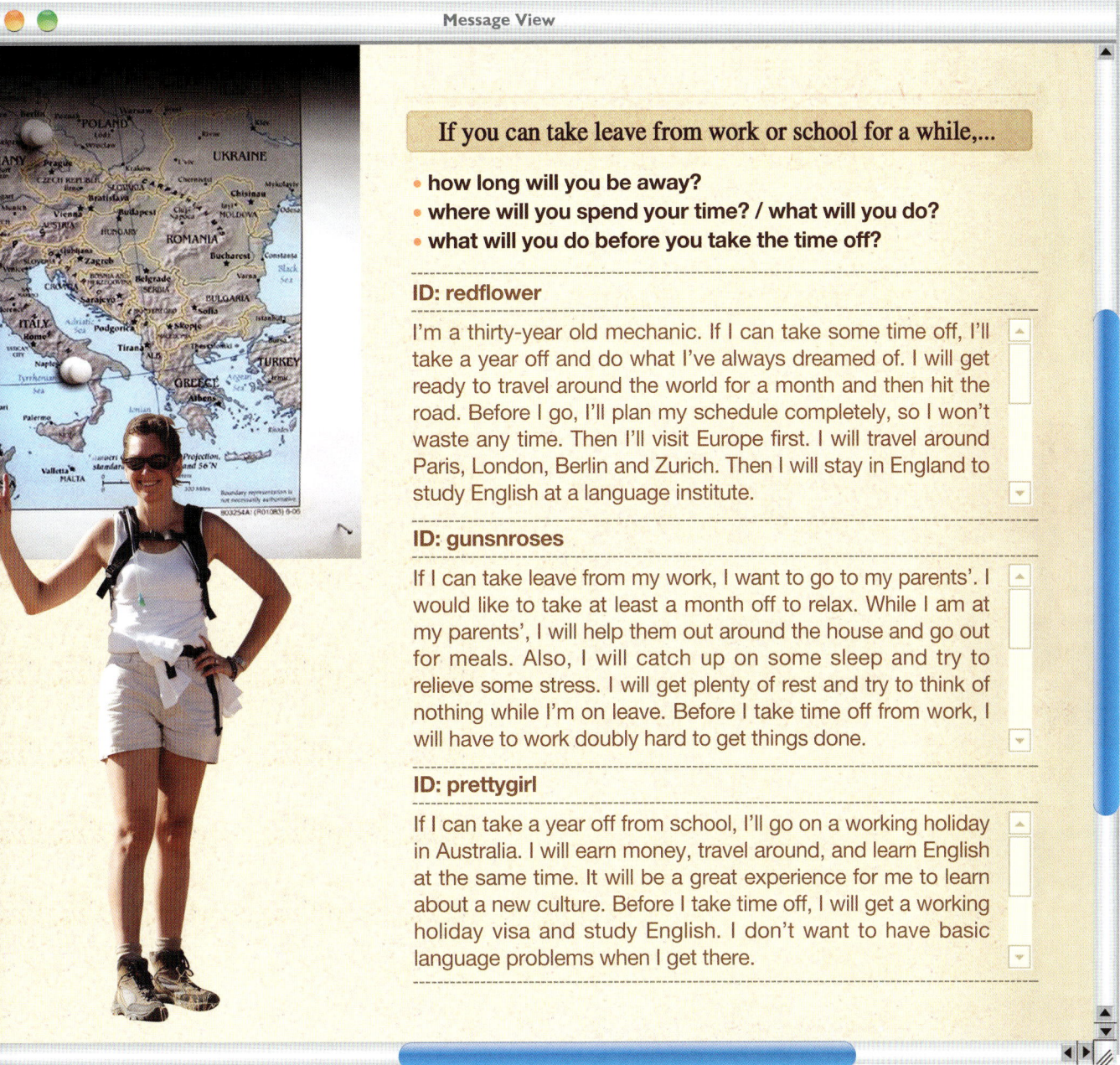

Message View

If you can take leave from work or school for a while,...

- how long will you be away?
- where will you spend your time? / what will you do?
- what will you do before you take the time off?

ID: redflower

I'm a thirty-year old mechanic. If I can take some time off, I'll take a year off and do what I've always dreamed of. I will get ready to travel around the world for a month and then hit the road. Before I go, I'll plan my schedule completely, so I won't waste any time. Then I'll visit Europe first. I will travel around Paris, London, Berlin and Zurich. Then I will stay in England to study English at a language institute.

ID: gunsnroses

If I can take leave from my work, I want to go to my parents'. I would like to take at least a month off to relax. While I am at my parents', I will help them out around the house and go out for meals. Also, I will catch up on some sleep and try to relieve some stress. I will get plenty of rest and try to think of nothing while I'm on leave. Before I take time off from work, I will have to work doubly hard to get things done.

ID: prettygirl

If I can take a year off from school, I'll go on a working holiday in Australia. I will earn money, travel around, and learn English at the same time. It will be a great experience for me to learn about a new culture. Before I take time off, I will get a working holiday visa and study English. I don't want to have basic language problems when I get there.

B. Discuss these questions with your partner.

1. Have you ever wanted to get away from what you do and take some time off? When do you feel like getting away from it all?

2. If you can take leave from work or school, how long will you be away?

3. If you can take leave from work or school, what will you do?

4. If you can take leave from work or school, what will you do before you go?

Writing

A. Pretend that you're backpacking around Europe. With your partner, talk about what you will do if you are in each of these situations.

1. What will you do if you get lost in a city?
2. What will you do if you run out of money?
3. What will you do if you can't communicate with the local people in English?

B. Write in detail about what you'll do in such situations. You may use the expressions given if needed.

1. What will you do if you get lost in a city?

- ask somebody on the street for help
- call the police
- look at the map of the area
- just wonder around

2. What will you do if you run out of money?

- ask parents to wire some money
- earn money
- borrow some money from friends
- stop traveling

3. What will you do if you can't communicate with the local people in English?

- get help from someone who can speak English
- learn the local language
- use body language

09 What is your ideal type?

Lesson Focus

- 01 Talking about relationships between men and women
- 02 Talking about the qualities of a good friend
- 03 Describing one's ideal type of man or woman
- 04 Using adjective clauses to describe one's ideal type

UNIT 09

What is your ideal type?

Get started

A. What's going on in this comic strip? Choose the correct words to describe each picture from the list and complete the sentence.

He had a _____ her.

He _____ her _____ on a date.

They started _____ with each other.

After a while, they _____.

They became _____.

They found they have _____ common.

- a lot in
- a couple
- going out
- crush on
- broke up
- asked out

B. The following statements are about friendship or romantic relationship. What do you think of each of them? Check if you think they are true or false.

	TRUE	FALSE
1 A friend is someone who talks behind your back.		
2 Men should always ask women out first.		
3 A relationship is based on respect and consideration.		
4 It is always good to break up a relationship by e-mail.		
5 Love at first sight never works out well.		
6 A healthy relationship needs a lot of effort.		

Talk together

Listen to the dialogue and practice.

Daniel: Hi, Kelly. How was the blind date yesterday? Are you going to see him again?

Kelly: Well... I don't know whether I am going to see him again. Actually, he's not my ideal type of guy.

Daniel: Hmm... What is your ideal type of man then?

Kelly: My ideal type of man is someone who is intelligent and has a lot in common with me. But, this guy was so different from me.

Daniel: I see. Do you want me to set up another blind date for you?

Kelly: Thanks, but it's OK. To be frank with you, I have a crush on someone.

Daniel: Wow, really? That's amazing! What do you see in him?

Kelly: He is quite close to my ideal type. I think he is the kind of man I could enjoy talking about various social issues with.

Language focus

What kind of person would you like to be friends with?	I'd like to be friends with someone who is honest and has a good sense of humor.
What do you think makes a good friend?	I think a good friend is someone who is loyal and honest. I think a good friend keeps promises and shares many things with me.
What is your ideal type of man / woman? What is your ideal type?	My ideal type of person is someone who has similar interests as me and understands me well.
What do you see in him / her? Do you believe in love at first sight? Do you think he / she is the right person for you?	He is hansome. / She is beautiful. Yes, I have a crush on someone. Yes, I think he is Mr. Right. / she is Miss Right.

Practice more

A. With your partner, talk about the kind of person you like as a friend using the words given.

- loyal, understanding
- Ryan
- loyal to friends, understands me well

- trustworthy, similar to me
- Jane
- keeps secrets, shares common interests with me

- funny, supportive
- Tom
- has good sense of humor, says nice things about me

Example

A: What kind of person would you like to be friends with?

B: I'd like to be friends with someone who is friendly and responsible.

A: Who is your best friend?

B: Adrian is my best friend.

A: What do you like about him?

B: He is really a nice person and he always keeps promises.

B. Work with a partner. Make conversations using the information in the questionnaire. Follow the example.

Questionnaire

❶ Do you believe in love at first sight?
❷ Are you seeing someone? If yes, who are you going out with?
❸ What do you see in him / her?

❶ yes ☑ no ☐
❷ yes ☑ no ☐ (Joy)
❸ thoughtful, loveable

❶ yes ☑ no ☐
❷ yes ☑ no ☐ (Chris)
❸ generous, positive

❶ yes ☐ no ☑
❷ yes ☑ no ☐ (Jennifer)
❸ understanding, has a lot in common with me

Example

A: Do you believe in love at first sight?

B: Yes, I do.

A: Are you seeing someone?

B: Yes. I'm going out with Andy.

A: What do you see in him?

B: He is kind and sincere.

Let's do it 1

A. What do you think most important things are when making new friends? Check (✓) what's important to you in your friendship.

- ☐ loyalty
- ☐ way of thinking
- ☐ trust
- ☐ honesty
- ☐ responsibility
- ☐ respect
- ☐ humor
- ☐ kindness
- ☐ affection
- ☐ appearance

B. Listen to people talking about the kind of person they'd like to be friends with and what they think a good friend should be like. Then complete the chart below.

	I'd like to be friends with...	A good friend is...

C. With your partner, talk about the kind of person you'd like to be friends with and what you think makes a good friend. Use the words in the chart above. Follow the example below.

Example

A: What kind of person would you like to be friends with?

B: I'd like to be friends with someone who is loyal and similar to me.

A: What do you think makes a good friend?

B: I think a good friend always takes my side and thinks the same way as me. And you? What do you think makes a good friend?

A: I think a good friend thinks positively and is supportive.

What is your ideal type? • 75

Let's do it 2 🎧

A. When it comes to romantic relationships, what do you think is the most important thing?
Listen to three women talking about their ideal types and find who is Mr. Right for each of them.

LOVE MATCH

	Ideal Type		**Ideal Type**	
Jane (24) waitress	* * *	● ●	* loving, caring, romantic girl * believes in love at first sight * wants someone who is about his age	John (30) athletic
Sarah (30) teacher	* * *	● ●	* independent and supportive girl * believes in destiny * wants someone who is much younger than him	Billy (32) doctor
Rachel (28) florist	* * *	● ●	* wants someone who has similar interests as him * doesn't believe in love at first sight * wants someone who is older than him	Scott (28) teacher

B. What is your ideal type like? Make a brief note about your ideal type.

My Ideal Type
*
*
*

C. Work in a group of four. Talk about your ideal types.

76 • UNIT 09

Reading

A. Do you think you can form a romantic relationship with a male/female friend? Let's check what some people think about this issue on a web article.

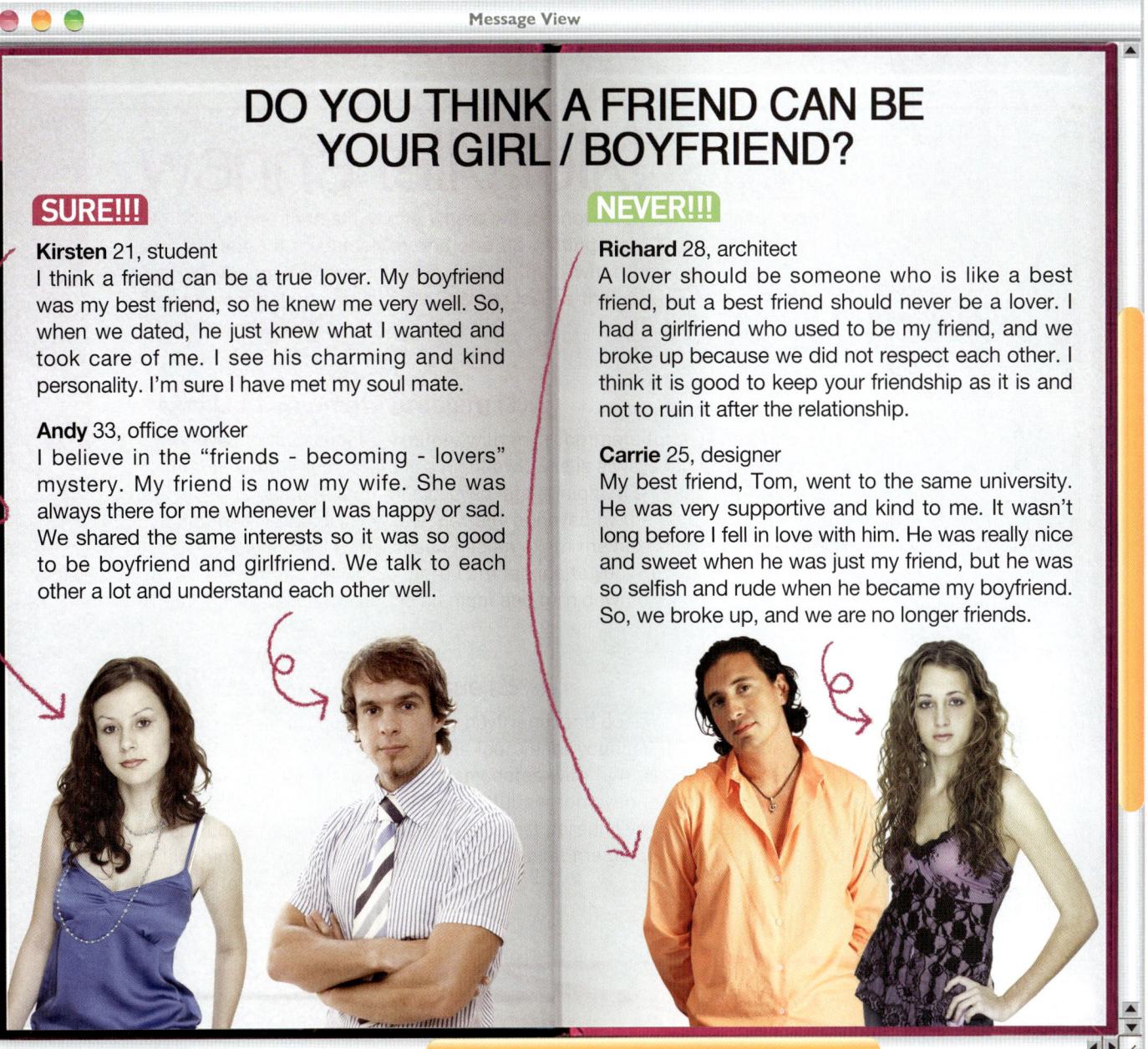

DO YOU THINK A FRIEND CAN BE YOUR GIRL / BOYFRIEND?

SURE!!!

Kirsten 21, student
I think a friend can be a true lover. My boyfriend was my best friend, so he knew me very well. So, when we dated, he just knew what I wanted and took care of me. I see his charming and kind personality. I'm sure I have met my soul mate.

Andy 33, office worker
I believe in the "friends - becoming - lovers" mystery. My friend is now my wife. She was always there for me whenever I was happy or sad. We shared the same interests so it was so good to be boyfriend and girlfriend. We talk to each other a lot and understand each other well.

NEVER!!!

Richard 28, architect
A lover should be someone who is like a best friend, but a best friend should never be a lover. I had a girlfriend who used to be my friend, and we broke up because we did not respect each other. I think it is good to keep your friendship as it is and not to ruin it after the relationship.

Carrie 25, designer
My best friend, Tom, went to the same university. He was very supportive and kind to me. It wasn't long before I fell in love with him. He was really nice and sweet when he was just my friend, but he was so selfish and rude when he became my boyfriend. So, we broke up, and we are no longer friends.

B. Discuss the following questions with your partner.

1. Why do Kirsten and Andy think we can be in romantic relationship with a friend?
2. Why do Richard and Carrie think that's impossible?
3. Have you dated a close friend or a best friend who is the opposite sex?
4. If yes, how did the relationship start? Was it a happy ending or a sad ending?
5. If no, do you think a friend can be a boy / girlfriend? If yes, why? If no, why not?

Writing

A. Most people like to hear or talk about first loves. Do you remember your first love? Or is the person you're seeing now your first love? Write about your first love. After you finish writing, share your stories with your classmates.

Example

I had my first love when I was an elementary school kid. One day, I saw a cute girl in front of the school library. I fell in love with her at first sight. I had a crush on her for 10 years, but I kept it a secret and acted like a good friend. When I became a university student, however, I finally asked her out on a date. To my surprise, she agreed to the date. We went to a movie, ate dinner and talked a lot. We had a lot of fun. Now, we are still happily seeing each other. I think I'm lucky to have her as my first love.

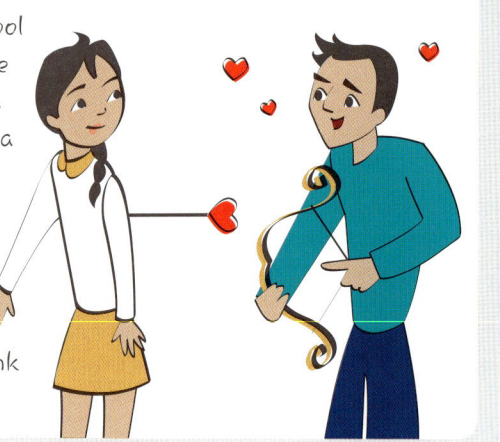

10 If you won the lottery, what would you do?

Lesson Focus

- 01 Talking about imaginary situations
- 02 Talking about wishes and dreams
- 03 Asking for and giving suggestions
- 04 Using the unreal conditional to talk about wishes and imaginary situations

If you won the lottery, what would you do?

Get started

A. Sally is daydreaming right now. Complete the sentences using the phrases below and match each picture with the correct sentence.

☐ If I won the lottery, I would _____.   ☐ If I were a famous star, I would _____.
☐ If I were slimmer than now, I would _____.   ☐ If I had a boyfriend, I would _____.

- go to an amusement park with him
- travel around the world in a private jet
- buy a huge house
- wear mini skirts

B. Ben is thinking about his problems. He wants to ask for some suggestions. Complete each sentence to give him suggestions.

1. I'm overweight.
2. I don't have a girl friend.
3. I don't speak English well.
4. I can't quit smoking.

❶ If I were you, I would _____   ❸ If I were you, I would _____
❷ If I were you, I would _____   ❹ If I were you, I would _____

- take English lessons every day
- exercise regularly and have a balanced diet
- join various kinds of social clubs
- try using a nicotine patch

Talk together 🎧

Listen to the dialogue and practice.

Ryan: Hi, Heather! I bought some lottery tickets today, and I am hoping to win one of these.

Heather: You what? Playing the lottery is gambling! Your chances of wining are one in a million!

Ryan: I know that. But, sometimes I like to gamble just to try my luck.

Heather: I wouldn't do that if I were you. If I had money to buy lottery tickets, I would save it.

Ryan: Don't be so critical! What would you do if I won?

Heather: I'd tap dance on a table in the cafeteria if you won. By the way, just for fun, what would you do if you won the lottery?

Ryan: If I won, I would buy a luxury sports car to travel around. Just thinking about it makes me so happy. What about you? What would you do if you won the lottery?

Heather: I would probably buy all the books in the bookstore.

Ryan: I could picture that.

Language focus

Unreal Conditional

What would you do if you found a treasure map?

If you were younger than now, what would you like to do?

Would you travel around the world if you won the lottery?

If I found a treasure map, I would/could sail to the treasure island.

I'd go back to school to study harder if I were younger than now.

No, I wouldn't. I would buy a brand new sports car if I won the lottery.

Making Suggestions

Brian asked me out. If you were me, what would you do?

I didn't hand in my assignment on time. What should I do?

If I were you, I would go out with him. He's a really nice guy.

If I were you, I would ask the professor for an extension.

Practice more

A. Match the sentences on the left with the corresponding future dreams on the right. Then make dialogues like the example below.

I wish I had a boyfriend. — go on a date with him every weekend

I want to be smarter.

He dreams of being a doctor. — look after sick people

She wants to get a passport. — enjoy working hard

He hopes to have the right job for him. — pass the bar exam

— travel around the world

Example

A: I wish I had a boyfriend.

B: What would you do if you had a boyfriend?

A: I would go on a date with him every weekend.

B. Match the problems on the left with the proper suggestions on the right. Then make dialogues like the example below.

Problems	Suggestions
I won't be able to finish this paper by tomorrow.	wear the pink dress you wore at your sister's wedding
I have no idea what to wear to the prom.	ask the professor for an extension
My co-worker asked me out on a date.	surprise her with some flowers
I am not ready for the presentation tomorrow.	go out for dinner and see what he(she) is like
My girlfriend was upset at me yesterday.	don't worry about it too much and try your best

Example

A: I won't be able to finish this paper by tomorrow.

B: If I were you, I would ask the professor for an extension.

Let's do it 1

A. If you were in the following situations, what would you do? Take turns with your partner asking and answering questions like the example below. You may use the expressions given when answering the questions.

Situations	Expressions	
You are locked out.	call the police / a locksmith / neighbors	break the window
You find $100 on the street.	find the owner	spend it all yourself
You are ten years younger.	go on many blind dates	study harder
A snake gets into your house.	date as many guys / girls as possible	go back to school
	ask someone for help	kill it by myself

Example

A: What would you do if <u>you were locked out of your house</u>?

B: <u>I would call a locksmith.</u>

B. Work with a partner. Take turns asking and answering questions using the phrases like the example below. And find out if you are either a realistic person or a dreamer.

Example

A: If you were locked out, would you break the window?

B: No, I wouldn't. I would call a locksmith. / Yes, I would break the window.

If you won the lottery, what would you do? • 83

Let's do it 2

A. Listen to people talking about job hunting and interviews. Fill in the table below.

Conversation	Problems	Suggestions
1		
2		
3		
4		

B-①. Imagine you are a job-hunting consultant and you are giving advice to a job seeker after a trial interview. Fill in the blanks in the problems column of the chart based on the evaluation sheet.

Things to improve
- arrives late
- has a weak voice
- lacks self-confidence
- lacks preparation
- can't speak English well

Problems	Suggestions
arrive late	arrive ten minutes early

B-②. As a consultant, you are giving the job seeker some advice. Write the advice you would give to the person in the suggestions column of the chart. Use the phrases given below. Then take turns with your partner making the suggestions.

- study English harder
- prepare what you are going to say
- speak clearly
- arrive ten minutes early
- have confidence in yourself

You arrived late for the interview. If I were you, I would arrive ten minutes early.

Reading

A. Have you ever dreamed of being a millionaire? What would you do if you became a millionaire? Read what some Netizens say about this in a web forum.

Message View

File(F)　Edit(E)　View(V)　Tools(T)　Message(M)　Help(H)

Web Forum

Welcome to the "Web Forum" for everyone. By joining our free community, you'll be able to post, discuss and reply to topics, participate in polls, and access many other features. Feel free to join in our "Web Forum."

✱ **What would you do if you became a millionaire?** << on: June 03, Joy

Post Reply

• **Re: Travel around the world**　<< June 06, Crystalclear

I would travel around the world if I became a millionaire. My dream is to travel around Europe and East Asia to see ancient artifacts. If I had the chance to go to East Asia, I would go to Hong Kong and then to Thailand. I'd like to see what life of Hong Kong is like, and I would like to shop as well. Then I would like to see the bright and splendid golden castle in Thailand. Oh... if only there was a chance of becoming a millionaire, I would do everything.

• **Re: Quit my job**　<< June 07, Etbelly

If I became a millionaire, the first thing I would do is to quit my current job and spend the time for my family and me. I would buy a nice house for my parents in a peaceful and clean area. Also, I would buy a car for myself. Then, I would save the rest of the money in a bank for later. ☺

• **Re: Build a private school**　<< June 09, Energizer

I would do the same thing that Etbelly would do if I became a millionaire. But, instead of saving the money in the bank, I would build a private school for little kids to learn English. Then I would be the principal of the school and would hire my younger brother as the vice-principal. I think this is such a nice future plan if only I had a million dollars in my pocket.

• **Re: Wow!!!!**　<< June 10, Lifesaver

Oh, my goodness! Just thinking about it makes me so happy.☺ If I became a millionaire, I would buy real estate in Hawaii and learn how to invest my money. I could invest the 1,000,000 dollars to make it grow. Then, I would quit my job. No more stress! I would live my life with my family and with millions of dollars if I won the lottery.

B. Discuss the following questions with your partner.

❶ After reading the replies, whose opinion is similar to yours?

❷ How are Energizer and Etbelly's plans similar?

❸ What do you think you need to do to become a millionaire?

❹ What would you do if you were a millionaire?

Writing

A. From time to time, we think about what it would be like if our dreams came true. What would you do if you were in the situations below? Write about what you would do.

Example

What would you do if you were 10 years younger?

If I were 10 years younger, I would study much harder in order to get into medical school. If I could turn back time, I would never skip classes to go out and play with my friends. I would become a doctor and help sick people.

What would you do...?

1 if you found a suitcase on the street that was filled with gold

2 if you were an invisible person

3 if you made a time machine and could travel to the future

11 Could you tell me the way to the bank?

Lesson Focus

01 Talking about locations of places
02 Asking for and giving directions to places
03 Asking and answering about the distance to a place
04 Asking for and making recommendations
05 Using imperatives to give directions

UNIT 11 Could you tell me the way to the bank?

Get started

A. What does each of the pictures say? Match each picture with the correct phrase.

☐ walk along the river ☐ go past the pet shop ☐ opposite the church
☐ turn left ☐ go straight ☐ go over the bridge

❶    ❷    ❸

❹ 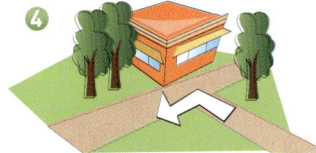   ❺    ❻

B. Complete the sentences and dialogue looking at the map.

❶ The bank is _____ the police station.
❷ The supermarket is _____ the hotel.
❸ The pharmacy is _____ the shoe store.
❹ A: Excuse me. Is there a movie theater near here?   B: Yes, there is one _____ the park.
❺ A: How can I get to the park?   B: Go _____ and turn _____ at the second corner. It's _____ the bank.

Talk together 🎧

Listen to the dialogue and practice.

Lucy:	Excuse me. Is there an Ace Bank around here?
Policeman:	Yes, there is one in the shopping mall.
Lucy:	How can I get there? I'm new here.
Policeman:	Cross the road and turn left. Follow that street until you get to the first traffic light. You will see the shopping mall on your right. The bank is on the first floor of the mall.
Lucy:	How far is it from here?
Policeman:	It's only about a five-minute walk from here. I can draw a map for you if you wish. You are now in the West part of the downtown and the shopping mall is in the North East. Here's a round sketch of the area. You can't miss it.
Lucy:	Great. Thanks a lot.
Policeman:	You're welcome.

Language focus

Asking about locations	Answering about locations
Is there a bank around/near here? Could you tell me where the bank is?	Yes, there's one next to / across from / in front of / behind the hotel. No, there aren't any banks near here. It's on Willow Street next to the library. It's on the corner of First Avenue and Palm Street.

Asking for directions	Giving directions
Could you tell me how to get to the bank? Can you tell me the way to the bank? How can I get to the bank?	Cross / Go across the road. Go straight for two blocks / 100m. Walk up / down this street until you get to the bank. Turn left / right (Make a left / right) at the first corner.

Asking about distance	Answering about distance
How far is it from here? How long does it take to get there?	It's within walking distance. It's about a five-minute walk away / from here. It's only a ten-minute walk.

Practice more

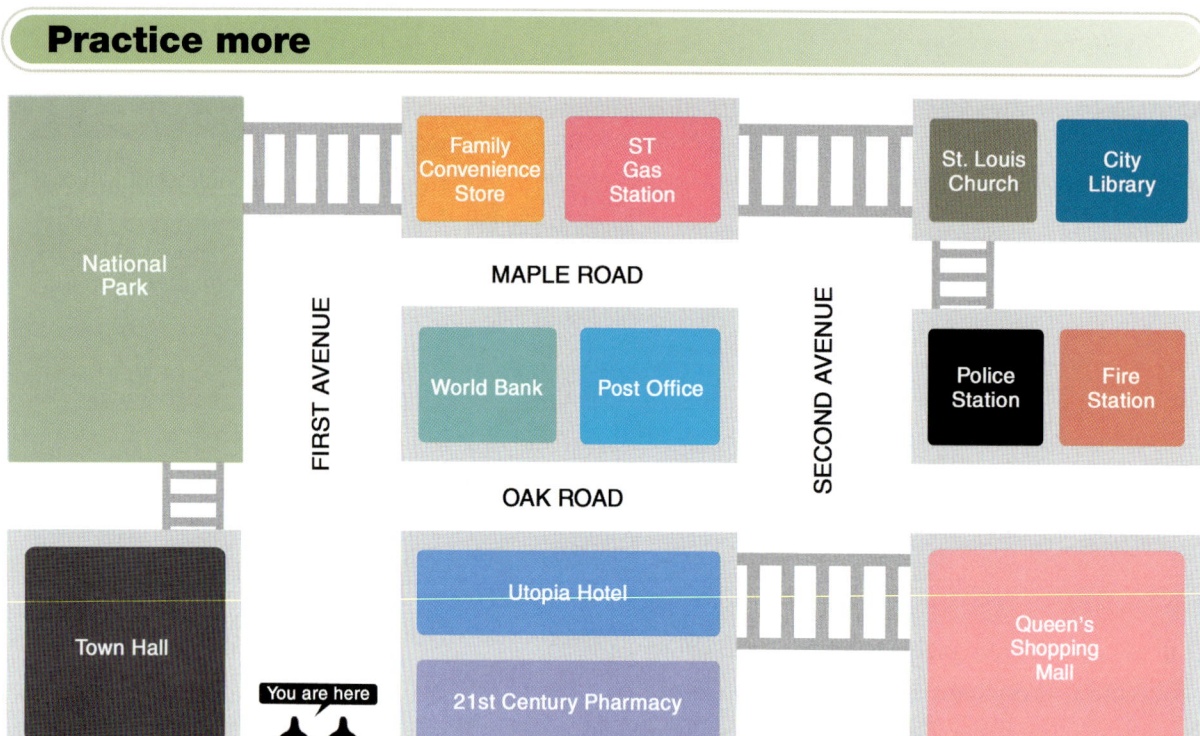

A. Work with a partner looking at the map above. Practice asking and answering about locations of the places in the list.

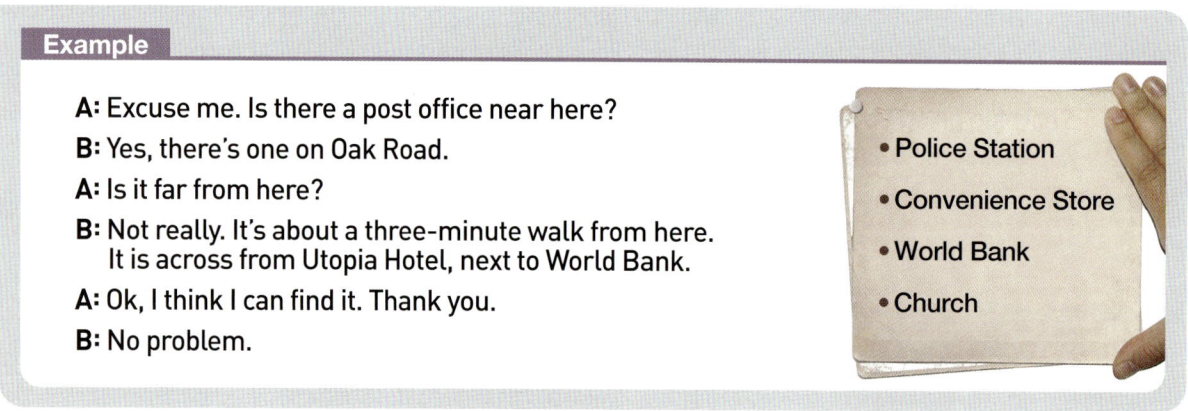

Example

A: Excuse me. Is there a post office near here?
B: Yes, there's one on Oak Road.
A: Is it far from here?
B: Not really. It's about a three-minute walk from here. It is across from Utopia Hotel, next to World Bank.
A: Ok, I think I can find it. Thank you.
B: No problem.

- Police Station
- Convenience Store
- World Bank
- Church

B. Work with a partner looking at the map above. Practice asking for and giving directions to the places in the list.

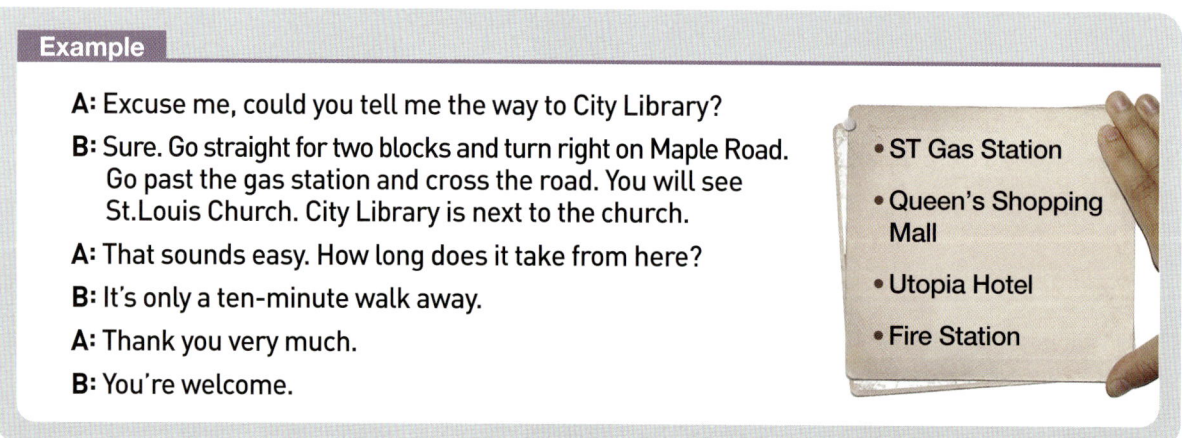

Example

A: Excuse me, could you tell me the way to City Library?
B: Sure. Go straight for two blocks and turn right on Maple Road. Go past the gas station and cross the road. You will see St.Louis Church. City Library is next to the church.
A: That sounds easy. How long does it take from here?
B: It's only a ten-minute walk away.
A: Thank you very much.
B: You're welcome.

- ST Gas Station
- Queen's Shopping Mall
- Utopia Hotel
- Fire Station

Let's do it 1

A. Imagine you're working as a receptionist for a tourist information center located in the downtown area of your city. Tourists are asking you for information. Make recommendations and fill in the chart below.

Places	Names of the places	Locations
a place for a quick breakfast		
a place for shopping		
a place for watching movies		

B. Listen to four conversations between friends. While listening, fill in the chart below and locate the places on the map.

	Places	Names of the places
1		Hardy's
2		
3	second-hand store	
4		

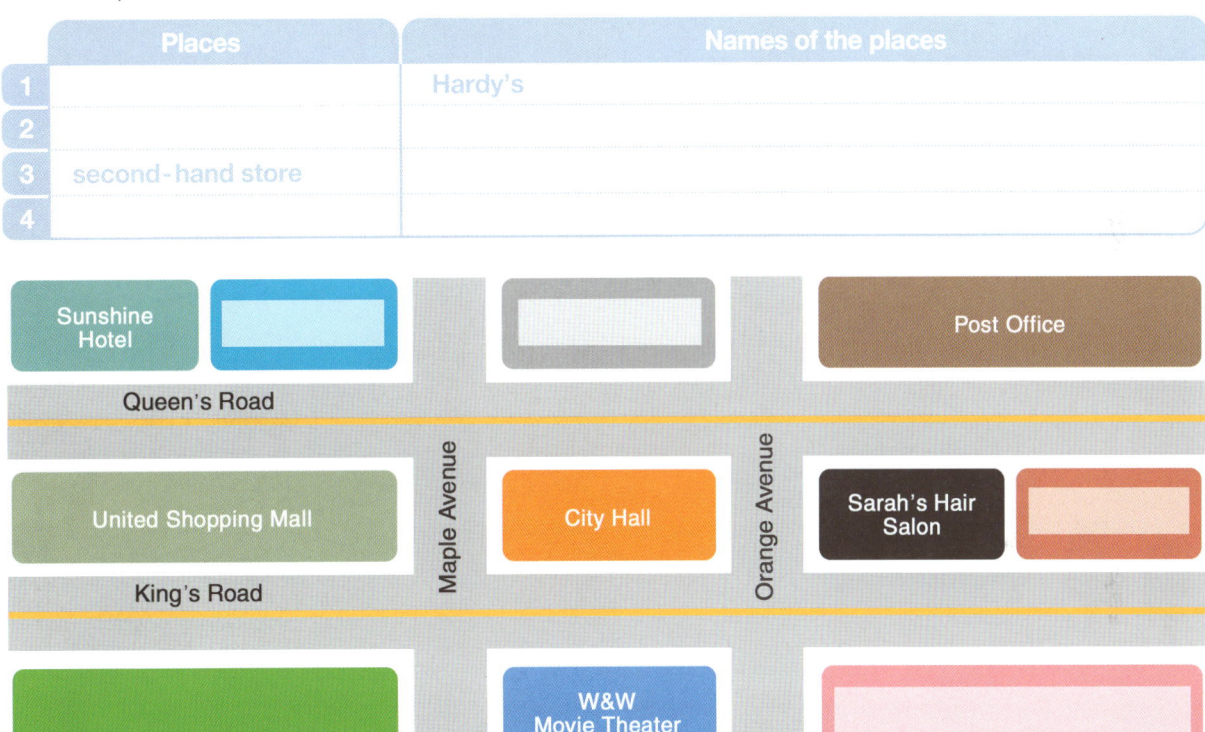

C. With your partner, make up dialogues using the information in the charts in Part **A** and Part **B**. Follow the example below.

> **Example**
>
> A: Excuse me. Do you know any good place for a quick breakfast?
> B: Have you tried *Olive's* Sandwich?
> A: No, I haven't. Are they good?
> B: Absolutely! They have the best sandwiches in town.
> A: Could you tell me where it is?
> B: Sure, it's close to Main Park Station. It's right next to Max Mart.
> A: Great! Thank you!
>
>

Let's do it 2

A. Listen to the conversations. Locate the places mentioned in the conversations on the map. Put the number of each place on the right blank.

① Jody's Hair Salon
② Endless Dental Clinic
③ Nihao Noodles
④ Grand Performing Arts Center

B. Imagine you are lost and standing in front of the tennis court. Make up dialogues with your partner about asking for and giving directions to the places other than those you located in Part **A** on the map. You may refer to the example below or the scripts in Part **A**.

Example

A: Excuse me. I think I am lost. Could you tell me how to get to Paradise Shopping Mall?

B: Sure. Follow 39th Avenue and go over the bridge. When you get to Cranberry Street, turn left. Then you will see a huge shopping mall right in front of you.

A: Thank you so much.

Reading

A. When you visit a new place for the first time, you can get information from a tourist map on how to get around. This is the map of the Riverwalk area, a famous tourist spot in San Antonio, Texas. Look at the information on some attractions to visit.

Attractions

① The Alamo

The historical district of The Alamo is located in the east end of Alamo Plaza and is beautifully landscaped. The remaining chapel and Long Barracks remain in their original locations. The area is now a museum with a compound and fortress for tourists. Come and meet the spirits of the Battle of the Alamo. Admission is free.

② Buckhorn Saloon & Museum

It has been voted as the "2002 Best Attraction" in San Antonio and is world-renowned. It is decorated in the traditional Texas style and has the most exotic collections you've ever seen. If you want to see a two-headed calf and a lamb with eight legs, this is the place! It is located three blocks from The Alamo.

③ La Villita

This is a historic arts village that has a collection of art objects, a shopping area and restaurants. It is located along the Riverwalk. Enjoy looking at various artifacts for free.

B. Discuss these questions with your partner.

① Of those three attractions, which one would you like to visit? Why?

② Imagine you are standing in front of The Alamo. You want to go to the convention center. How would you get there? Explain how to get there to your partner.

③ Are there any places in your neighborhood that you'd like to recommend to newcomers or visitors? What are the places and where are they?

Writing

A. You might have your usual places to go shopping for good bargains. Think of one of those places. It could be an outlet store, a clothing shop, a grocery store, etc. Write the directions on how to get to that place. Include the reasons why you visit that place often.

Example

When I go clothes shopping, I usually go to Merry-Go-Round. They have a good selection of quality clothes and accessories, and the salespeople are very friendly. Actually, the thing I like best about Merry-Go-Round is the low prices. Besides, people say that they like the clothes that I buy from this store. The store is on Chester Avenue. To get there, you should take the subway and get off at Baker Station. When you walk out of the station, turn left and go down the hill until you get to Sunflower Shopping Center. Merry-Go-Round is on the second floor of the shopping center. It's between the bookstore and the gift shop.

12 Where do you go to school?

Lesson Focus

01 Talking about various fields of study
02 Talking about how to register for courses in college
03 Talking about kinds of schools and degrees or diplomas
04 Talking about educational systems in different countries
05 Talking about plans regarding education

UNIT 12 Where do you go to school?

Get started

A. What subjects do you study at high schools? Put each subject in the appropriate category.

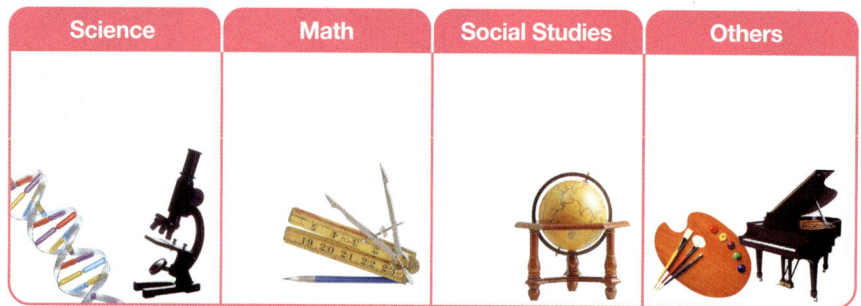

Discuss these questions with your partner.
1. Which subject do you like the best? Why?
2. Choose one subject you don't like to study. Why don't you like it?
3. Which subject do you think is useful in your life? What is the reason?

B- 1. There are various fields of study at university. What did you study? What are you studying? What would you like to study? Put the majors in the list in the appropriate category.

Humanities

Social Science

Natural / Applied Science

- Sociology
- International Relations
- Literature
- Chemistry
- Economics
- Geology
- Engineering
- Astronomy
- Linguistics
- Political Science
- Psychology
- Art History

B- 2. Complete the sentences with the proper words from the above list.

1. _____ is the study of the stars, planets and other natural objects in space.
2. I'd like to study more about the importance of the community and how society works. In that case, I need to be a _____ major.
3. I've decided to go abroad to study _____. I want to study how languages work.
4. Kate is working at an art gallery. Her major at university was _____.

Talk together 🎧

Listen to the dialogue and practice.

Nick: Hi, Sarah.
Sarah: So how is your university application process going?
Nick: Actually, I got accepted at three of the universities, but I haven't decided which one I'm going to.
Sarah: You wanted to go to college on the East Coast.
Didn't you get into any universities there?
Nick: Yeah, but, I can't decide between these two; a private college in Virginia and New York University.
Sarah: Wow, it sounds like you don't even have to think about it. Why don't you go to New York University?
Nick: Well, it's a well-known school. However, if I go to the private college, they will offer me a full scholarship and financial aid for my graduate studies.
Sarah: Oh, I see. That would be a good opportunity for you.
You've wanted to go to medical school, then you will need financial support.
Nick: Right! That's why I'm more into the private college.
Sarah: Good luck with your decision.

Language focus

What school do you go to? Where do you go to school (college)?	I go to Emory High School. I go to the University of Clova.
What grade are you in? What year are you in?	I'm in the eighth grade. I'm a freshman / sophomore / junior / senior.
What do you study? What is your major?	I study chemistry. I am a psychology major.
Why do you study biology? Did you get accepted anywhere?	I study biology to get into medical school. I got accepted by three universities. I got admitted to three universities.
What courses are you taking this semester?	I'm taking geography and psychology this semester.

Where do you go to school? • 97

Practice more

A. With your partner, practice the dialogue below by changing the underlined parts with the given majors.

A: Hi, Samantha. What's up?
B: Hi, Jack. Wow, we both attend this university.
A: Oh, I didn't know that. So, what do you study (what is your major)?
B: I study psychology. What about you?
A: Oh, actually I am an economics major. (I major in economics.)
B: Do you? My second major is economics too.

- English Literature
- Mathematics
- Accounting
- Physics
- Psychology
- Communication
- Anthropology
- Spanish
- Education
- Chemistry
- Geography
- Music history

B. With your partner, practice the dialogue below by changing the underlined parts with your own words.

At high school

A: How are things going at school?
B: Pretty good.
A: By the way, what school do you go to?
B: I go to Orinda High School.
A: And what grade are you in?
B: I'm in the 10th grade.
A: So, do you enjoy your school life there?
B: Yeah, I get along well with my classmates.

At college/university

A: Where do you go to college?
B: I go to Jefferson College.
A: What year are you in?
B: I'm a sophomore.
A: And what do you study?
B: I am a nursing major.
A: How do you like studying there?
B: I like it very much.

C. With your partner, practice this dialogue by changing the underlined parts with the given expressions.

A: Hey, how is your university application process going?
B: You know what? I got accepted by Emory University.
A: Wow, great. So, what do you plan to study?
B: I'm going to study social work.
A: Why would you like to study social work?
B: I'd like to help people in need.

- Did you get accepted anywhere?
- Chemistry - invent 100% natural cosmetics
- Psychology - study the human mind
- Chinese - do business with China
- Education - be a school counselor

Let's do it 1

A. All college students need to register for the classes they're going to take for a new semester. Fill in the class registration form by using the list of general education requirement courses. After that, compare the form with your partner's.

General Education Requirement Course List for 2007 Spring

Code	Course Title	Time	Credits
ENGL110	College Composition I	MWF 10:00~10:50	3
MATH165	Calculus I	MWF 15:00~15:50	3
BIOL126	Human Biology	TT 9:00~10:50	3
ART111	Introduction to Art History	TT 11:00~11:50	2
COMM110	Fundamentals of Public Speaking	WF 17:00~17:50	2
PHYS110/L	Introductory Astronomy/Lab	MWF 8:00~8:50	3
HIST101	Western Civilization	MF 13:00~13:50	2

Class Registration Form

Student I.D	Last Name	First Name	Code	Course Title	Time	Credit

Address	Phone#	E-Mail

Total Credits

B. Listen to people talking about classes at university and check (✓) whether the following statements are true or false.

		True	False
Conversation 1	1 Melinda wants to re-register for the class.		
	2 Professor Handon is willing to sign the drop card.		
Conversation 2	1 Eu-jin hasn't decided which master's program to take yet.		
	2 Jim will graduate next spring if he passes the biochemistry class.		
Conversation 3	1 Martin needs to take more credits due to failing a calculus course.		
	2 Sue hasn't completed her general education requirements.		

C. Work with your partner. Make up dialogues like the example below using the words in Part **A** and your own words as well.

> **Example**
>
> A: Hi, how many classes are you taking this semester?
>
> B: I only need to take ten credits. So, I'm taking four classes. How about you?
>
> A: You're lucky! I need to take 12 credits this semester. So I am taking College Composition I, Calculus I, Introduction to Art History, Western Civilization, and Fundamentals of Public Speaking.
>
> B: I'm also taking Fundamentals of Public Speaking and Western Civilization. I'll see you in the classes then.

Let's do it 2

A. Match the kinds of schools with the diplomas / degrees you get there.

- vocational school • • Certificate
- community college (2-year college) • • MA / MS / Ph.D
- university • • AA / AS
- graduate school • • BA / BS

B. What do these people want to do? Listen to people talking about their study plans and fill in the blanks.

	Conversation		Diploma / Degree	Field
1		Ashley		
		Ryan		
2		Mark		
		Christina		
3		Jason		
		Kelly		

C. With your partner, make up dialogues like the example below. You may use the listening scripts in Part **B** and the phrases given in the box.

Example

A: What do you want to do after graduating from high school?
B: I want to go to a vocational school.
A: What for?
B: I'd like to be a fashion designer. I think it's better to get a certificate first. How about you?
A: I applied to several colleges to study biology.
B: That sounds cool.
A: I already got accepted by the University of Harrington.
B: Congratulations!

- take a break from studying
- get the job I want
- apply to colleges / universities
- get a certificate in...
- get into a graduate program
- go to a vocational school / community college

Reading

A. What is the educational system like in your country? Below are the educational systems of three different countries. Compare them with your country's.

Education in the U.S. is provided mainly by the government. People are required to attend school until the ages of 16 to 18, depending on the state. Many more states now require people to attend school until the age of 18. Students may attend public, private, or home schools. In most public and private schools, education is divided into three levels: elementary school, junior high school, and senior high school. Grade levels in each vary from area to area.

In China, to provide its population with education, it has a vast and varied school system. There are preschools (kindergartens), primary schools, secondary schools, and various institutions of higher learning consisting of regular colleges and universities, professional colleges, and short-term vocational universities. China's system looks like a pyramid. Student numbers decrease sharply at the higher levels.

In Germany, optional kindergarten education is provided for all children between the ages of three and six years old. Primary education usually lasts for four years. In contrast, secondary education includes four types of schools based on a pupil's ability as decided by teacher recommendations. A special system of 'Job Training' called 'Duale Ausbildung' allows pupils in vocational training to learn in a company as well as in a state-run school.

B. Discuss the following questions with your partner.

1. What is your country's education system like?
2. Which country's educational system is close to your country's? How are they same? How are they different?
3. What are the good things about each country's educational system?
4. Which country's educational system do you think is most practical? Why?
5. Which country do you like to study in? Why?

Writing

A. These days, people get various kinds of education and training based on their choice and needs throughout their lives. Choose one of the questions below and write a short passage about it.

1. If you go to college in the future, what do you want to study?
2. If you plan to go back to college, what would you like to study? Why?
3. If you want to get a special training, what do you want to get trained in?
4. If you'd like to get a higher or another degree, what degree would you like to get? In what field? Why?

Example

I'd like to get into a graduate program in web design. I've worked as a web designer for three years since I graduated from university. But, I think I need to get trained in creating better designs. I wasn't an art or design major as an undergraduate. So when I have a hard time getting ideas on design, I feel that I need to learn more on how to create good designs.

Wanna Talk 3
Listening Script

UNIT 01 — What is she like?

Let's do it 1

A. Austin and Sarah are friends from back in high school. They are looking at their school yearbook while thinking back on the good old days. Listen to the conversation and label each person with his / her name.

Conversation 1

Austin: Wow! Sarah. Are you looking at a high school yearbook?
Sarah: Yup! I'm remembering the good old days, but it seems that I can't really remember some of the people in the pictures.
Austin: Really? I might remember them because I tried to keep in touch with the people I met in high school.
Sarah: That's great! Look at this picture, Austin. Who is this tall and muscular guy with sunglasses on?
Austin: The one wearing jeans and white sleeveless T-shirt?
Sarah: Yes. He looks cool with short blond hair.
Austin: Yeah. His name is Tyler. He was the student body president in grade 12.
Sarah: Then, how about the one with pink shorts and a bikini top?
Austin: The one who is holding a beach ball? She's Melissa. She looked very cute in her shoulder-length curly black hair like this.
Sarah: She's quite plump and not so tall.
Austin: Yeah, but still looks cute. Tyler and Melissa were a couple at that time, but not anymore.
Sarah: Oh, I see. Hmm... who is this guy? He looks like he is in his mid-40s. The one with ivory colored pants and a flowery Hawaiian style shirt.
Austin: You mean this guy who is short and quite overweight? His name is Nick. He was the top student in my class. Oh, wow! Here's Nicole! I went out with her.
Sarah: Nicole? Who's she? Is she the tall and skinny looking girl?
Austin: Yeah, the one with an orange dress and a beautiful straw hat.
Sarah: She has wonderful blue eyes and long blonde hair!
Austin: Yeah, she was amazing, but we haven't seen each other since we broke up.
Sarah: Oh, I am sorry. Hmm... Who is this boy with a blue cap?
Austin: The boy who is playing soccer?
Sarah: Yes, I like his sky blue shorts and striped T-shirt.
Austin: His name is Kevin. He loved playing all sorts of sports. That's why he was so well-built.
Sarah: Wow! It's always very interesting to look at old pictures.

Let's do it 2

B. Listen to the descriptions of four people and fill in the table with the proper words from the list.

Description 1

Professor Anderson doesn't allow students to hand in their papers late. He also tells students that he will lock the back door when the class starts. So, students who are late will have to come in the front door and suffer the embarrassment. But, his classes always fill up on the first day of registration because he gives the greatest lectures to students. He works in his professor office until late doing research.

Description 2

Ray, who is my friend from high school, is a very special guy. He is always the top student in every class. He is especially good at math, so he participated in a math competition when he was in high school. He got second place at that time. Ray also likes to try something hard to challenge himself, so he often goes mountain climbing. He says that someday he would like to join an expedition to climb up Mountain Everest.

Description 3

I've never met anybody who knows so many jokes and knows how to make people laugh like Andy. Andy is my co-worker and I have known him for three years. He puts little notes on the photocopier every day for people to have a look at. The notes say things that make people happy and motivate them. He also knows a lot of funny jokes, so he is known as an office clown.

Description 4

I want to tell you about my mom. My mom is like my best friend. I tell her everything about my school life and even about my relationship issues. She listens to me carefully and sometimes gives me advice. She has a strong maternal instinct so she cares about me a lot. Also, she does some charity work once a week to help poor people. I love my mom very much.

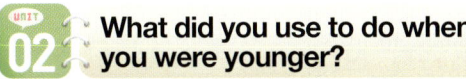 What did you use to do when you were younger?

Let's do it 1

B. People are talking about the things they used to do. Listen to three conversations. Then put the number of the conversation next to the correct activity.

Conversation 1

A: What did you used to do when you were a kid?
B: I used to play hide and seek in the playground. I remember that I always got dirty and got many scratches from playing games. What about you? What did you used to do when you were a kid?
A: Well, I used to play baseball at school. I even had a baseball uniform. I always wore it to school. I think I got less interested after I entered high school.
B: Why? What did you like to do after you became a high school student, then?
A: I liked to go scuba diving because my family moved to a beautiful house that was a 5-minute walk from the beach.
B: Wow! You were so lucky. I used to play with my pets in my front yard when I was a teenager because my family loved having pets at home.

Conversation 2

A: What did you used to do when you were in university?
B: I used to enjoy night outs with my friends a lot. We also went camping on a beach. I was kind of wild. What did you used to do after you graduated from high school, Craig?
A: Hmm... Compared to you, I was laid-back. I used to like jazz so much that I listened to it everyday.
B: Jazz? I never listen to jazz. What made you like jazz music?
A: After I entered a university, I used to work a part-time job in a record shop. I listened to music while I was working and I instantly fell in love with jazz. But, I can't listen to jazz anymore. I got tired of it.
B: Oh, what a pity!

Conversation 3

A: Hey! You look very happy. What did you do last weekend?
B: Oh, I went to see the Philharmonic Orchestra on Saturday. I really enjoyed it
A: Wow, sounds great. What did you enjoy about it?
B: Well, it reminded me of when I was a teenager. I used to play the violin and my dream was to be a violinist. I stopped playing the violin after I started high school. What did you used to do when you were a teenager?

A: I used to read a lot of comic books. I almost read a hundred of them! I wanted to be a comic-book writer when I was a teenager. But, my parents wanted me to study hard and become a reporter.
B: You can still read comic books as a hobby now, just as I often go to the orchestra to remind me of my younger days.

Let's do it 2

B. Listen to three TV talk show clips. The host is talking to three guests about their personal histories. Check if the statements below are True or False.

Clip 1

Host: OK, today, we are with the author of the best-selling novel, 'The Hero', Kimberly Johnson.
Johnson: Hello, everyone. Thank you very much for inviting me here.
Host: Welcome, Kimberly. Your book 'The Hero' has been a best seller for 2 months now. So, could you tell me how you started writing novels?
Johnson: Well, when I was a teenager, I loved to read novels. I tried to read 4 novels a week. If I didn't have the time to read, then I read the bible. When I was fed up with just reading, I imagined things a lot. Then, I started to write on a little scrap paper about what I imagined. These slowly became my stories. It was the start, I guess.
Host: How old were you then?
Johnson: I was 15.
Host: Wow, I see. So, is 'The Hero' your first published novel?
Johnson: As a matter of fact, it is not. Before gaining success from 'The Hero', I failed a lot of times. I think I wrote more than 50 novels. Half of them were never published and the other half were published, but failed commercially.
Host: Wow, I can't believe it. I'm reading 'The Hero' at the moment, and it is really touching. You have such a delicate writing style.
Johnson: Thank you very much.
Host: Could you say a word to the teenagers or people who are dreaming of becoming novelists?
Johnson: If you are dreaming of being a writer, never give up!
Host: Nice advice. We'll be back after this commercial break.

Clip 2

Host: Let's welcome today's guest, a world-famous chef, Nick Murray. He is the first place winner in the 48th annual French Cuisine Contest.
Murray: Thanks for the warm welcome. Nice to meet you all.
Host: You're a chef at a five-star hotel. Could you share with us about your school days? What were you like?

Murray: When I was a college student, I majored in French history. But then, I was more fascinated by French cuisine than the history. So, I worked hard at a steel factory to earn enough money to go to France. I traveled in France during my summer vacation to experience the food culture and to taste the original cuisine. While I was there, I decided to be a chef.

Host: Wow, you have such an interesting past. Could you talk about it more? What did you do after you traveled?

Murray: After I came back, I enrolled in a cooking class. So, I went to university to study French in the morning and then I went to a cooking class at night.

Host: Oh... Did you become a famous chef right after your university graduation?

Murray: Actually, it took some time. I got a job as an assistant chef at a tiny little restaurant. I want to say this to the young audience here, "Don't be afraid of starting from the bottom!"

Host: I have a lot of respect for you. It has been a long journey until you are here now.

Clip 3

Host: Today, I have a special guest in the studio. He is the world-renouned fashion designer, Tim Oliver. Let's welcome him on the studio.

Oliver: Thank you, thank you so much.

Host: Every woman wants to wear your clothes, Tim. Look! I am wearing your clothes now. What do you think about this?

Oliver: I'm so honored to be loved by many women, especially by you. Haha.

Host: What did you study when you were in university? I heard you studied something different from fashion design, is that right?

Oliver: Yeah, that's right. I majored in construction in university.

Host: Then what made you change your mind and become a fashion designer?

Oliver: When I was a university student, every friend of mine was rich, so they bought a lot of fashionable and cool clothes. But, I couldn't. So, I decided to fix my old clothes and make new clothes for myself. After that, I started altering my clothes to suit my own style. My friends told me that I looked so nice and trendy. So I began to make clothes for my friends as well.

Host: How about your construction studies? Didn't you like studying construction?

Oliver: I thought that a university degree was not that important if you have other interests and abilities. So, I dropped out of school.

Host: I see. So, what did you do after you dropped out of school?

Oliver: I started a fashion business with the help of my rich friends.

Host: You can tell us more about the fashion business after the break. Stay tuned!

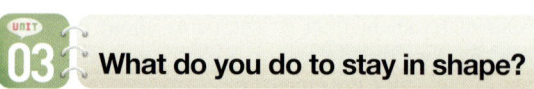

What do you do to stay in shape?

Let's do it 1

B. Do you think John is in shape? What about Tracy? Talk to your partner about what advice you'd like to give to them.

Conversation 1

John: Hi, Tracy. Wow, you look stunning!

Tracy: Do I? Thanks. Maybe it's because I started taking care of my health a bit more.

John: Tell me about it. What do you do to keep fit?

Tracy: I just do some exercises and have a healthy diet. How about you? Don't you do anything to stay healthy?

John: Actually, I don't do anything in particular. But, I think I should start doing something, otherwise I will be out of shape.

Tracy: Then why don't you start doing simple exercises like stretching, taking a walk, and so on?

John: Right, so I just started working out at the gym two weeks ago. So, I tried to go to the gym twice a week. And you? How many times a week do you exercise?

Tracy: Well. I go jogging by the river at least four times a week.

John: Wow, it must be hard to do exercise that often. And what is your diet like?

Tracy: I can't eat any kinds of fast food at all. And I try to have at least five servings of fruit and vegetables every day. What do you usually eat?

John: I enjoy having meat, pizza, and hamburgers. I know they are not good for my heath, but I can't help it.

Tracy: Well, you should change your eating habits. Try to cut down on meat and junk food and eat more healthy food.

John: Yeah, I'll try. I think I should go get some fruit and vegetables right now so that I can start a healthy diet from now on.

Let's do it 2

A. Jesse and Laura are talking about the things they do to stay fit. Listen and fill in the chart with the kinds of exercises they do and the food they eat.

① Hi, my name is Jesse. I want to focus on two things in order to stay healthy: regular exercise and healthy eating habits. Firstly, on weekdays, I spend about 50 minutes at the gym. I usually do some stretching and run on the treadmill. Then, on the weekends, I spend time with my family. We usually play sports together like tennis and badminton. We go hiking every other Sunday. In order to maintain a healthy lifestyle, I also try to eat the right kinds of food. I try not to eat fattening food, junk food or fast food. Instead, I eat a lot of vegetables, fish and fruit. I have spinach, tomatoes and bananas almost everyday.

② Hi, my name is Laura. I want to tell you how I lost 20 pounds in two months. My doctor said that I really needed to think about my weight because it caused my health problem. His advice was to cut down on fattening foods and junk food such as chocolates cheese cake and hamburgers. Also, he told me to exercise at least three times a week. I've followed what he told me to do for two months and here I am now. I always wake up at 6 o'clock every morning and jog for an hour. Also I try to drink a lot of water. I drink at least six glasses of water a day. When it comes to eating, I have low calorie and high fiber food and rarely eat meat and food containing transfat. Even though I don't really like eating vegetables, I have nothing but a bowl of salad with vinegar dressing for dinner everyday. So, my diet plans has made me who I am now.

What do you do when you're bored?

Let's do it 1

A. Listen to people talking about how they feel now. Choose the proper word from the list that describes how each of them is feeling now.

B. Listen again. Complete the sentences about why they feel that way.

Mike: I was typing my report for five hours and all of a sudden my computer broke down. It happens sometimes, but why today? This report is due tomorrow afternoon. I immediately turned off the computer and turned it back on, hoping the report file would not be gone. However, nothing appeared on the monitor. I couldn't figure out what the problem was. The work that I had been doing so far was gone. Now, I have to type it out all over again. I feel like I am about to explode!

Allison: I lied to my parents this morning. The reason why I lied was because I really wanted to go rafting with my friends on the weekend. But, my parents do not allow me to go rafting because they think it's dangerous, especially because I can't swim. So, I told them that I would be away at a design workshop on the weekend. They gladly allowed me to go there. I feel bad about it, but if I didn't lie, I wouldn't be able to go rafting with my friends.

Claire: There is a guy who is in my photography class. He kept looking at me and talking to me during class. Then he asked me for my phone number. He called me last weekend and asked me whether I wanted to go and see a movie. I said OK. We watched a movie and ate dinner. He was really sweet and generous that day, but the next day in class, he neither talked to me nor looked at me. He acted very strange. I don't know why he changed so suddenly.

Tom: I went to a fair that was held in the Olympic stadium. And, you wouldn't imagine what I did a few days ago. I went bungee jumping! I always wanted to go bungee jumping but I didn't have time. I jumped off a 236m high crane. When I stepped up on the platform and looked down, it was higher than I thought. It is really hard to explain how it felt when I stepped off the platform. I felt like I was an eagle. I can still feel my heart beating. It was just great!

Kenneth: This morning I took the subway to work. It was so crowded that I could hardly breathe. When I got to work, I discovered that I had lost my wallet. I had my I.D card and credit cards inside my wallet. Also, the wallet was brand new and expensive. I just bought it last week! But in the afternoon, I received a phone call from a police officer telling me that he found my wallet. Later, they told me that someone found it and handed I over to the police. I think I got lucky.

Gwen: I have been studying for my final exam and presentation for the last three months. I got a D on my Marketing mid-term which really surprised me. So, I am doing my best to study hard for my final exams and the presentation that I have to make next week. I am sure that I will pass the final and get a good grade on my presentation. I have been to the library so many times to do research and study, and I dropped by the professor's office to ask questions. I think I am ready for the exam and presentation.

Let's do it 2

B. Listen to people talking about what they usually do when they're in certain moods and complete the chart.

① Somebody was trying to break the lock on my door yesterday. My heart was beating so hard that I couldn't even speak. I almost fell down because my legs were shaking so hard, but I called the police. After a short while, policemen caught the thief and neighbors helped me calm down. Whenever I think of that moment, I try to do something else, such as yoga and listening to music. These things help me calm down a little bit.

② I just found out that my friend, who I thought trusted, has talked about me behind my back. I can't believe he did that to me. I hoped it was some kind of misunderstanding. So, I will call him and talk things through. I will ask him what made him do that and what I did wrong. I think talking it over with the person is the best way to solve the problem. Then I usually forget about this kind of bad feeling by playing basketball or soccer.

③ I am so mad at my boss. He didn't allow me to go on an important business trip because I am female. Instead of me, a male co-worker went on the business

Listening Script • 107

trip. Can you believe it? I should have gone because I put together the presentation. When I feel this way, I hang out with my friends, have a few drinks and go to a Karaoke bar to feel better.

④ My boyfriend took me to a nice, romantic restaurant this evening. He dressed so well and acted like a gentleman. I wondered why he took me to such a lovely restaurant even though it wasn't my birthday. After dinner, a dessert came out with a shiny, diamond ring beside a rose. He kneeled down and proposed to me. Tears kept running down my cheeks and I was smiling. When I feel such deep emotions, I usually start crying and treasure the memory forever.

UNIT 05 · Have you ever gone bungee jumping?

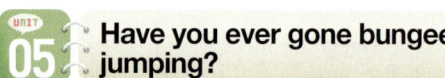

B. Listen to people talking about their experiences and complete sentences by filling in the blanks.

Conversation 1

Michelle: Have you ever gone bungee-jumping?
Nick: Yes, I have.
Michelle: Wow, how many times have you done that?
Nick: Three times so far, but every time I did it, I felt scared.
Michelle: Oh, did you? Then how come you've done it three times then?
Nick: Feeling scared sometimes helps relieve stress, just like watching horror movies in summer to cool yourself off.
Michelle: Oh, interesting. So where did you do that for the first time?
Nick: In New Zealand. Two years ago when I worked at the branch office. How about you? Have you ever gone bungee-jumping?
Michelle: No, not yet, but I've wanted to do that for a long time. Actually, I like to try doing extreme sports. I have gone water-rafting, hang gliding, rock climbing, etcetra.
Nick: Then, I'm sure you'll definitely feel very exited about doing that.
Michelle: Yeah, I think so. I'm planning to go to the Sunshine Coast next month for my first try.
Nick: Fantastic! You'll love it!

Conversation 2

Helen: Have you ever tried Turkish food?
Ken: Uh-huh, many times.
Helen: Oh, so what dishes have you eaten?
Ken: I've mostly had Kebab, the most popular, typical Turkish cuisine. How about you? Have you ever tried Turkish food?
Helen: No, I haven't, but I have tried other kinds of foreign food like Mexican, Indian, Cuban, etcetra.
Ken: Then, do you like Burritos?
Helen: Yes, Burritos are one of my favorites. I often have them for lunch. Anyway, I've never had Turkish food before, I'd like to try some.
Ken: Oh, there's a good Turkish restaurant that serves authentic Turkish food made by Turkish cooks. How about having lunch there sometime next week?
Helen: That sounds good. I'd like to try some Kebabs.

Conversation 3

Megan: Honey, I've been thinking about where to go for our summer vacation. Have you ever been to a tropical island?
Bill: Yeah, I've been to Indonesia on a business trip. So would you like to go to a tropical island?
Megan: Sort of. As you know, I like traveling, but I've only been to countries with historical sites.
Bill: So where have you been?
Megan: I've been to India, Turkey, and Greece. So this time I'd like to go to a place good to relax.
Bill: Then, what about going to Bali? There are some historical sites worth visiting as well as luxurious resorts to relax in.
Megan: Sounds perfect, by the way, haven't you been to Bali? You said you've been to Indonesia.
Bill: No, I haven't. I just visited the capital city.
Megan: OK. Bali sounds good to me. We've been working hard and I'm fed up with our routine. We need to have some relaxation time on the beach.

Let's do it 2

B. Listen to three interview clips. After listening, check(√) if each of the following sentences is true or false. If the sentence is false, correct it.

Clip 1

Host: Hello, everyone. Can you guess who is here today? I'm really happy to introduce one of the top TV stars, Jennifer Norman!
Jennifer: Thank you for your warm welcome.
Host: They say that you've been seeing someone and are planning to get married soon. Could you tell us about this? You look like you are in love!
Jennifer: Ha ha! Yeah, I'm in love and going out with... as you know... Ken Wagner.
Host: You mean, the rock musician, Ken Wagner?
Jennifer: That's right.
Host: Oh, that's wonderful. How long have you been going out with him?
Jennifer: We've been together for nine months now.
Host: How did you meet, may I ask?
Jennifer: Sure, it's not a big secret. I have been one of his big fans for many years and I went to his concert the other day. After the concert, I went backstage, and we just fell in love at the first sight.
Host: How romantic!

Clip 2

Reporter: Hello, Mr. Dickson. I'm a reporter from the company magazine.
Mark: Hello, nice to meet you.
Reporter: I'm going to write an article about your being selected the Employee of the Year. So, can I ask you a few questions?
Mark: Sure.
Reporter: First, congratulations on getting the Employee of the year award.
Mark: Thank you. Actually, I haven't done anything particular. I've done just what I'm supposed to do.
Reporter: I guess you're a very humble guy. So how long have you been working for this company?
Mark: Let me think... It has been almost 20 years since I started working in the sales department.
Reporter: I know it's not the first time for you to get this award. How many times have you gotten the award?
Mark: You know, many times. Ha ha... actually this is the third time.
Reporter: What do you think makes you an excellent employee?
Mark: That's the question I keep asking myself. Every time I get this award, I ask myself if I have worked hard enough to deserve this award.

Clip 3

Reporter: How are you? Susan. I'm Lisa Jung from Woman's Fitness. Thanks for being here for today's interview.
Susan: Hello, nice to meet you.
Reporter: Your figure is great! You look healthy and gorgeous.
Susan: Thank you.
Reporter: First, may I ask your age? I've heard that you're in your thirties.
Susan: Sort of. Actually, I just turned 40 last month.
Reporter: Pardon? You're 40? You look like you're in your twenties! What is your secret to keeping fit and staying young?
Susan: I don't do anything special. I just exercise regularly and eat healthy.
Reporter: What kinds of exercises have you done these days?
Susan: I've been power-walking and going hiking on the weekend.
Reporter: How long have you been doing that?
Susan: For about five years since I moved to this town.
Reporter: And your diet. What is it like?
Susan: Actually I haven't been on a special diet, but I've been a vegetarian for about three years.

UNIT 06 What's the purpose of your trip?

Let's do it 1

B. Listen to four phone conversations between guests and hotel staff. Then fill in the table below.

Conversation 1

A: Hello. Can I help you?
B: Hello. Can I talk to the person who is in charge of the heating system?
A: You can talk to me. What's the matter?
B: I think there is a problem with the heating system in my room. I can't seem to get the heat on and there is no hot water.
A: What room are you in?
B: I'm in room 503.
A: Oh! I'm terribly sorry for this inconvenience. The heating system on your floor is out of order. Everyone is being informed about this.
B: But, I can't stand it. It's freezing in here.
A: The only thing we can do right now is to change your room to another room.
B: That sounds better. I'd like to move to another room right now.

Conversation 2

A: Hello, what can I help you with?
B: Hi, I'm in Room 302. Can I get Internet access in this room?
A: Oh, I'm sorry. We do not offer the Internet access in single rooms.
B: Then how can I use the Internet? I have to use it to prepare for a business meeting.
A: I see. Do you have your own laptop with you?
B: Yes.
A: Then for a small charge, you can connect the telephone adapter to your laptop and access the Internet that way.
B: Oh, no. Will I be charged extra? And accessing the Internet will be very slow, right?
A: I'm afraid that is true. Or, you can change the room to a double room. There is free Internet access in every double room.
B: Hmm... I will call you back after I think about it.

Conversation 3

A: Good afternoon. May I help you?
B: Yes, I'd like to order room service for my breakfast.
A: OK. We offer three types of breakfast: American, Continental, and Asian-style. Which type would you like to order?
B: I think I will go for the American breakfast.
A: Our American breakfast includes cereal, bacon, eggs, sausages, tomatoes, toast, and tea or coffee. Would that be alright?
B: That sounds great.
A: Ok. What time do you want to be served?
B: 8:00 am will be perfect.
A: Anything else?
B: And, I'd like fresh orange juice instead of tea or coffee.
A: Sure, no problem.

Conversation 4

A: Sunnydale Hotel. How may I help you?
B: I'm in room 805 and I just checked in, but I think I was given the wrong room.
A: Hmm... you are Mr. Murphy, right?
B: Yes. When I reserved the hotel room, I asked for an ocean-view room. But, my room faces the mountain.
A: I am sorry, Mr. Murphy. All of the ocean-view rooms are booked. That's why we upgraded your room to a suite and sent you an apology.
B: We would still like to have an ocean-view room.
A: Then we can move you to an ocean-view room as soon as we have a vacancy.
B: When will we get an ocean-view room, then?
A: The earliest will be tomorrow afternoon.
B: OK. Give us a call then.

Let's do it 2

B. A couple, who is going to get married soon, plan to spend five days and four nights in Bali for their honeymoon. Listen to their conversation and complete their itinerary.

Julia: Have you been thinking about where we will go for our honeymoon?
Alex: Yes, I have. There are so many places that people go to for their honeymoons.
Julia: Right. The Maldives, Bali, Cebu, Fiji, etc. They all provide similar honeymoon packages. So, it's hard to decide which one we should take for our honeymoon.
Alex: Honey, how about Bali? We can spend five days and four nights there. There are many modernized hotels in Bali with reasonable rates.
Julia: What is there to do in Bali?
Alex: Here is my plan. On the first day, we arrive at the Bali Heaven Hotel, and then go relax on the beach. I heard that the scenery near the resort is breathtaking. And, we could also celebrate our marriage in the beach cocktail bar. The next day, we can take part in all sorts of marine sports, such as go scuba diving, surfing and sea-walking.
Julia: Sounds really fun! I would really like to go scuba diving. When do we go for a massage, then? I want to get a massage to relax.
Alex: On the third day. We will go white water rafting. Then, when we feel tired, we will go get a massage and go for some spa treatments.
Julia: Sounds like paradise to me! I can't wait to go there.
Alex: There's more. On the forth day, we will go paragliding. I've always wanted to try it. And, we will take a lot of pictures.
Julia: Wow! This is unbelievable! You've made a great plan, honey!
Alex: On the last day, we will do some shopping and take one of the free tours. After that, we will depart. How's the plan?
Julia: Couldn't be better. Thanks for putting this all together.
Alex: My pleasure!

UNIT 07 Could you get me some water?

Let's do it 1

B. Listen to the conversations and fill in the chart. Write reasons if the request is refused.

Conversation 1

A: My hands are full. Would you mind making ten copies of this material?
B: I don't mind at all, but unfortunately the photocopier is not working.
A: Oh, no. I really need them right now. Could you call someone to fix it?
B: Sure. I'll do that immediately.

Conversation 2

A: My friend is getting married this evening at City hall.
B: Wow! That's near my house.
A: Really? Then could you give me a ride on your way home today?
B: I'm sorry. I won't be going home straight after work. I have plans with my friends.
A: Oh, that's fine. I can take the subway.

Conversation 3

A: Janet, your music is so loud that I can't concentrate. Would you mind turning the volume down a little bit?
B: Of course not. I didn't know the music was so loud. Sorry about that.
A: Thanks. By the way, what were you listening to? Could I borrow your CD sometime?
B: Sure. It's a brand new single by Christina Aguilera.

Conversation 4

A: I'm stuck with a bunch of reports to finish today. Ryan, would you mind faxing this for me?
B: You've asked the wrong person. I am really bad at handling machines. Why don't you ask Jon to fax this for you?
A: I wish. But, he's taken a day off today.
B: Oh, no. I'm sorry I can't be of any help.

Let's do it 2

A. Peter, who is a college student, has been talking to the people below to ask for permission. Listen to the conversations and number the pictures.

Conversation 1

Peter: Excuse me. Is this seat taken?
Stranger: It is empty right now, but I am saving it for my friend.
Peter: Oh, I see. Then could I sit here until your friend comes? I need to eat my lunch but all tables are occupied.
Stranger: Sure, go ahead. My friend won't be here for a while, anyway.
Peter: Thanks.

Conversation 2

Peter: Good morning, Professor. Could I talk to you for a minute?
Professor: Of course. Come on in. What do you want to see me for?
Peter: I was going to take the Chemistry 101 class that you're teaching, but the class is already full. So, I can't register. Would it be possible for me to sit in on the class?
Professor: That won't be a problem. But since you're auditing the class, you won't be able to take part in discussion sessions. Would that be fine with you?
Peter: Sure. Thank you very much.

Conversation 3

Librarian: Good morning. May I help you?
Peter: Oh, yes. These books are due today, but I really need them for my final paper. So, would it be possible for me to get an extension?
Librarian: Let me see. May I have your student I.D.?
Peter: Here you are.
Librarian: Hmm... I am sorry. You have already extended the due date once. Since there are students who have reserved these books, you are not allowed to take any more extensions.
Peter: Oh, no... In that case, am I allowed to photocopy some of them?
Librarian: Sure, as long as you keep the reference.

Conversation 4

Peter: Hey, Tom. Do you have an MP3 player that has a voice recording function?
Tom: Yes, I do. What's up?
Peter: Good. I need to record an interview for my Psychology class, but I don't want to carry my huge voice recorder. May I borrow your MP3 player?
Tom: When do you need it?
Peter: I need it next week. Monday to Friday.
Tom: Oh, no. I can't lend it to you for the whole week. I need to listen to it as well, Peter, so that I can practice for my band.
Peter: I see. Then, would you mind if I use it from Monday to Wednesday?
Tom: I'm sorry. I really need it for practicing my band's music.

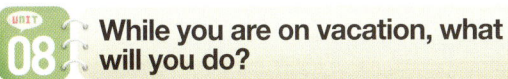

UNIT 08 While you are on vacation, what will you do?

Let's do it 1

B. Listen to people talking about their plans and complete the sentences below.

Conversation 1

Denise: Cathy. Have you decided what you will you do if you get a week off?
Cathy: Well, I will either take a scuba diving lesson or learn how to in-line skate.
Denise: Hmm... which would you like to do more?
Cathy: Well, it's hard to decide, but I think I'm going for the scuba diving. I think it's going to be more challenging than in-line skating.
Denise: Yeah, scuba diving sounds more challenging to me, too.
Cathy: How about you, Denise? What will you do if you get a week off?
Denise: Hmm... I will probably get some rest at home to relieve stress from work. I will read the books that I've always wanted to read and sleep as much as I want.
Cathy: Is that it?
Denise: Yup! I like to have relaxation time and do nothing.

Conversation 2

Amanda: Kelly, are you going somewhere after this semester ends?
Kelly: Oh, I'm going to visit my friend in Hong Kong. I'm so excited!
Amanda: Sounds fun, so, when are you leaving?
Kelly: Actually I'm working on a paper, and the deadline is the 15th. I'm planning to leave right after I'm done with it. I don't think I'll have a problem getting a seat on the plane around that time.
Amanda: Right. What will you do while you are there?
Kelly: I will go shopping and enjoy the gorgeous night scenery in Hong Kong. Also, while I am there, I will eat a lot of dimsum. What about you, Amanda? What will you do while you're off from school?
Amanda: Oh, I will go to see my brother's family. I haven't seen them for a long time.
Kelly: I see. Then, what will you do while you're staying with them?
Amanda: Well, I will play with my little nephews and take a look around my brother's farm.
Kelly: Sounds like a good plan.

Conversation 3

Melissa: Hey, it's almost time to call it a day. Do you have any plans?
Jim: Nope, nothing in particular. I'll probably go straight home. What about you? What will you do after work?

Listening Script • 111

Melissa: I'll go to see the outdoor concert performed by the City Orchestra.
Jim: Oh, will you? By the way, it's Tuesday, isn't it?
Melissa: Right, Why?
Jim: I almost forgot to go to the hip-pop dance class I'm taking on Tuesdays and Thursdays.
Melissa: Wow, you're taking a dance class? That's surprising. So will you go to the class after you get off?
Jim: Sure, I wouldn't miss it for the world. That's one of the ways I can keep fit. So where will the concert be held?
Melissa: At City Square in front of City Hall. It's free and will be held every Tuesday throughout the month.
Jim: Really? I like going to classical music concerts, so I'll go to see it before it ends. Could you tell what time it starts?
Melissa: It starts at 7:30. If you like Mozart, you should go next Tuesday. They will play Mozart's pieces.

Let's do it 2

B. Listen to the conversations and check(✓) if the invitation was accepted or refused. If the invitation was refused, write down the reasons.

Conversation 1

John: Hello, Gwen. Are you doing anything special this week?
Gwen: Not really. Why?
John: Well, it says on the campus bulletin board that there will be a magic lesson on Tuesday. Would you like to go with me? It will be a lot of fun.
Gwen: What time on Tuesday?
John: It's a two-hour session, starting from 1 to 3 pm, Tuesday, the 5th at Main Theater. It says that it's free of charge, but you need to bring your own cards.
Gwen: Hmm... I'm not really sure.
John: Why? You are not interested in magic tricks?
Gwen: It's not that I don't like magic tricks. I'd love to go, but I might have to go to see my advisor around 2 p.m. But, I'm not sure yet, so I'll let you know if I can make it to the lesson.
John: OK. I hope you can make it.

Conversation 2

Eddie: Hey, Brooke! Congratulations on your graduation. You've finally made it!
Brooke: Thanks! I couldn't have made it without your help and support.
Eddie: You don't have to say that. By the way, I heard that there'll be the graduation exhibition. Will your art pieces be displayed as well?
Brooke: Yup! My sculpture will be there. It's called 'Platonic Love.'
Eddie: Ooh~! I look forward to seeing it. Well, when is the exhibition?
Brooke: It's from June 18th to 22nd. So, will you come when you are free on one of those days?
Eddie: Certainly, I will go. Where will it be held?
Brooke: Oh, it will be in Rose Hall and open from 10 am to 4 pm.
Eddie: Alright. I will give you a ring on the day I plan to go.
Brooke: Thank you so much, Eddie.
Eddie: No problem.

Conversation 3

Derek: Wow! Check this out, Jessie.
Jessie: What's up?
Derek: There will be a hip-hop performance this Friday. It also says that there will be a dance and snack party after the performance. How great!
Jessie: Whoa-whoa. Calm yourself down. You are so upbeat.
Derek: Jessie, let's go and watch the performance. Then we can enjoy a dance party there as well.
Jessie: Hmm... how much is the entrance fee?
Derek: Let's see. Oh, it's $5. It's not that expensive.
Jessie: Well... I will have to learn how to groove before I go there. I dance like a stick. I don't want to make fool of myself on the dance floor.
Derek: Oh, don't worry. I'll teach you how to move to the music if you decide to go with me.
Jessie: Sure, I'd love to go.

Conversation 4

Will: Amy, when is your last final exam?
Amy: Tomorrow is my last exam. Thank goodness!
Will: Great! Then how about going on a cycling tour with me from the 13th to the 14th of June? What do you think?
Amy: A cycling tour? I can't even ride a bike. How am I supposed to go cycling?
Will: I'll teach you how to ride if you want to go. Come on! It will be fun! Besides, the fee is cheaper than any other summer program.
Amy: How much is it?
Will: It's $100, including meals and accommodation. The only thing you need to have is a bike.
Amy: Oh, I'm sorry, I can't. I don't even have my own bike. Above all, I am scared of riding on two wheels.
Will: Then, I guess I will have to find somebody else. Maybe next time?
Amy: Yes, I will let you know if there are any other good summer programs that I can share with you next time.

UNIT 09 What is your ideal type?

Let's do it 1

B. Listen to people talking about the kind of person they'd like to be friends with and what they think a good friend should be like. Then complete the chart below.

① I'd like to be friends with someone who is funny and supportive. My best friend is Ron. Ron and I have been best friends since we were in elementary school. He and I share many interests such as basketball and football. It is so much fun when he is around. So, I think a good friend is someone who has a good sense of humor and someone who is there for me when I go through hard times.

② I'd like to be friends with someone who is trustworthy and positive. My best friend's name is Cathy. She knows everything about me because I tell her everything. But, she never tells anybody about what I said. Also, she is so positive that she is always smiling. So, I think a good friend is someone who keeps promises and has positive thinking.

③ I'd like to be friends with someone who is kind and respectful. Anne is my best friend's name. She has such a wonderful personality. She always thinks about other people first. Also, she and I are very close to each other. We live next door, so we spend a lot of time hanging out and studying together. She always helps me do my assignments, as well. Therefore, I think a good friend is someone who always gives me a hand when I am in need and thinks the same way as me.

④ I'd like to be friends with someone who is both loyal and similar to me. Ben has been my best friend for 15 years. He thinks the same way as I do. Because we understand each other so well, sometimes there's no need for words between us. Ben and I are on the same ice hockey team at university, so we always practice together. So, I believe a good friend is someone who shares many things with me and who always takes my side.

Let's do it 2

A. When it comes to romantic relationships, what do you think is the most important thing? Listen to three women talking about their ideal types and find who is Mr. Right for each of them.

① I'm Jane, and I work as a waitress. My ideal type of person is someone who is intelligent and someone I can respect. I can be quite supportive whenever my boyfriend is tired and depressed. I sometimes believe in love at first sight, but I mostly believe in destiny. I think there is a perfect guy out there somewhere. I am attracted to someone who is a lot older than me so that he treats me like a lady. I wish I could find my true love.

② I'm Sarah and a 30-year-old teacher. My ideal type of person is someone who is similar to me and who can share the same interests as me. It would be great if he understands my job so that I could talk about it with him. I like someone who is close to me so that I feel comfortable being with him. I don't believe in love at first sight because I believe that love grows over time. I never used to be attracted to younger men, but these days, that seems to have changed.

③ I'm Rachel. I'm a florist. My ideal type of person is someone who is physically attractive and healthy. Honestly, when I first meet people, I notice their looks. That's why I believe in love at first sight. I could be lovable and sweet to my boyfriend. I could decorate things with flowers and throw a surprise party when my boyfriend is in a bad mood. I like someone who is close to my age so that we could be like best friends.

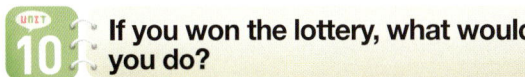

UNIT 10: If you won the lottery, what would you do?

Let's do it 2

A. Listen to people talking about job hunting and interviews. Fill in the table below.

Conversation 1

A: How are you doing?
B: Not so well, actually. I have been having a hard time finding a good job. I've sent resumes to almost 100 companies, but I haven't gotten a call back from any of them.
A: I'm sorry. But if I were you, I would not give up hope and I would try harder.
B: Thanks. I will keep that in mind.

Conversation 2

A: I have a job interview this Friday, and it's going to be in English. How can I prepare for this?
B: If I were you, I would ask for help from my English teacher and practice answering possible interview questions.
A: I wish I had more time. It's too late to start studying for an English interview.
B: Well begun is half done! It's never too late to start.

Conversation 3

A: I got a call from one of the companies I applied to.
B: That's great! Congratulations!
A: Thanks. Well... I have a job interview tomorrow, but I don't know what to wear.
B: If I were you, I would wear a dark colored suit and tie my hair up neatly.
A: Okay. I'll take your advice.

Conversation 4

A: Why do you look so depressed?
B: Oh, I had a job interview this morning, but I don't think I got the job.
A: What makes you think that?
B: I got so nervous in front of interviewers. My voice was shaking so bad and I didn't know what I was talking about.
A: That's OK. If I were you, I would just forget all about it and start preparing for more interviews.
B: Okay. I will try not to let it bother me.

UNIT 11: Could you tell me the way to the bank?

Let's do it 1

B. Listen to four conversations between friends. While listening, fill in the chart below and locate the places on the map.

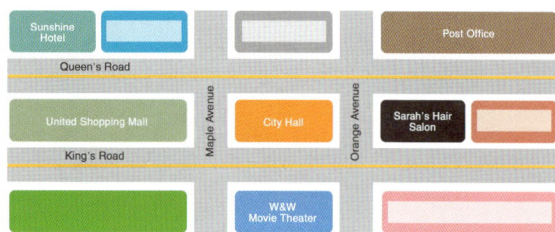

Conversation 1

(on the phone)
Jeff: Hello.
Amanda: Hi, Jeff. This is Amanda.
Jeff: Hi, Amanda. What's up?
Amanda: My doorknobs are so old that they got rusty. I need to get some new ones, but I don't know where I can get them.
Jeff: You can get them at Hardy's. It's a hardware store that is near City Hall.
Amanda: I see. But I don't know where City Hall is.
Jeff: Then do you know where the post office is?
Amanda: Ah, yes!
John: Good. Hardy's is across from the post office and opposite to City Hall. It's on Queen's road.

Conversation 2

Mayumi: Hey, Peter!
Peter: Oh, thank goodness! Mayumi, hi!
Mayumi: Why are you so surprised?
Peter: Oh, I am so glad that I bumped into you. I think I'm lost.
Mayumi: Why? Where were you heading?
Peter: I was looking for a car dealership. It's called.... Oh, I forgot! But, I heard that it's near here somewhere.
Mayumi: Aha! Are you looking for T-Car Station? The one across from CGB Movie Theater, right?
Peter: Exactly. Could you tell me where T-Car Station is?
Mayumi: Sure. Do you remember where you had a haircut the other day?
Peter: Yes. Sarah's Hair Salon.
Mayumi: Right. T-Car Station is on King's Road, opposite Sarah's Hair Salon.
Peter: Oh, I got it. Thanks!

Conversation 3

(on the phone)
Alex: Apple Tree. How may I help you?
Judi: Hi. I am wondering if you have some good quality second-hand furniture there.
Alex: Yes, we do. We have desks, sofas, TV tables and other pieces of furniture that are all in good condition.
Judi: Ok, I will come by with a friend of mine. Could you tell me how to get them? I am fairly new in this town.
Alex: Sure. Do you know where T-Car station is?
Judi: Not really, but I know where the movie theater is.
Alex: OK. T-Car station is right across from the theater. And, Apple Tree is across from T-Car station, next to Sarah's Hair Salon.
Judi: I think I got it. Thanks. I will be there around three.
Alex: O.K. I'll see you then. Bye.

Conversation 4

Jake: I'm starving. I think I could eat a horse.
Emily: Me, too. Wow! It's already 7:30.
Jake: Yeah. Shall we go for a nice dinner? What do you think?
Emily: I think that's a good idea. I want to have some steak.
Jake: Steak sounds good to me, too! Do you know of a place that serves good steak?
Emily: I know one on the corner of Queen's Road and Maple Avenue. It's called Royal Steakhouse.
Jake: Oh, you mean the one next to the Sunshine Hotel?
Emily: Exactly! Have you been there? The restaurant there is really fancy and nice.
Jake: I've never been there, but I saw it when I went to United Shopping Mall. It is near the mall, isn't it?
Emily: Right. Let's go there! I'm hungry.

Let's do it 2

A. Put the number of each place on the right blank.

Conversation 1

Amber: Oh, hi, Peter! What are you doing at the police station?
Peter: Hi! Hmm... I lost my wallet a few days ago and I got a call from the police saying that the owner of a Chinese restaurant found my wallet and is keeping it safe for me.
Amber: That's very nice. So, do you know the name of the Chinese restaurant?
Peter: It's called Nihao Noodles. But, the problem is that I don't really know where it is.
Amber: I think I know where it is. I've had dinner there before.
Peter: Really? Could you tell me how to get there?
Amber: Go right up Cranberry Street, pass the shopping mall and make a right. Go straight for one block. Then you will see a Japanese restaurant Kyoto Sushi. The Chinese restaurant is right past the Japanese restaurant.
Peter: I got it. Thanks a lot.

Conversation 2

(on the phone)
Jody: Hello. Jody's Hair Salon.
Jenna: Hello. I have an appointment to have my hair permed, but I don't know how to get there. I think I am lost.
Jody: Okay. Where are you now?
Jenna: I'm at the subway station right now. Can you tell me how to get there from here?
Jody: Sure. Can you see a bridge in front of you? First, go over that bridge and walk straight for about two blocks until you get to the stationery store. Then turn left. You will see our hair salon between Cool Stationary and Hollywood Photo Studio.
Jenna: How long does it take to get there from here?
Jody: It takes about five minutes or so.
Jenna: Okay. Thanks. I'll see you then.

Conversation 3

(on the phone)
Tom: Hello.
Helen: Hello. Tom, this is Helen. I'm sorry, I think I'm going to be late.
Tom: Oh, how late? The show will begin in ten minutes.
Helen: I know. But, I just got off from the bus, and I can't find anywhere to cross the river.
Tom: Oh, I see. Don't worry. So, you are at the bus stop now, right?
Helen: Right.
Tom: Helen, go left down Cranberry Street and pass Paradise shopping mall. You will find a bridge on the right hand side. Then cross the bridge and turn right, then walk along the riverside. You will see the entrance of Riverside Park. Go in and walk through the park. Then you'll see the Grand Art Performance Center on your right-hand side.
Helen: Okay. I see the bridge. How far is it from the bridge?
Tom: It only takes about five minutes if you walk fast. I'll be in front of the art performance center.
Helen: Okay, I'll see you in a minute. Bye.

Conversation 4

Sean: Mom, my tooth hurts. I can't bite into my ice-cream.
Mom: Oh, honey, I think you have a cavity. It's better to go and see a dentist as soon as possible, before it gets serious.
Sean: I don't know of any dental clinics around here.
Mom: Well, there is one on the opposite side of the river.
Sean: Really? Is it within walking distance?
Mom: Sure, it is. It's only about a ten-minute walk.
Sean: Where is it, mom?
Mom: When you leave the apartment complex, follow 39th Avenue to the bridge. Then go over the bridge and walk straight. Make a right on the corner of 39th Avenue and Elm Street. Go past the supermarket and you'll see it there. The name of the clinic is called Endless Dental Clinic. It's right next to the supermarket.
Sean: Could you draw a map for me?
Mom: Sure. Here it is. You can't miss it.

UNIT 12 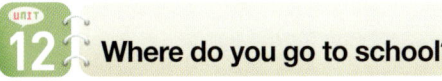 Where do you go to school?

Let's do it 1

B. Listen to people taking classes at university and check (✓) whether the following statements are true or false.

Conversation 1

Melinda: Hello, Professor. Handon. Could I have a talk with you for a moment?
Professor: No problem, Melinda. What would you like to talk about?
Melinda: Well, I've signed up for your Economics 200 class, but I don't think I can take it this semester.
Professor: That's too bad. May I ask the reason?
Melinda: My part-time working hours have changed. I've already missed class a couple of times since the semester started. I wonder if it's ok to drop the class.
Professor: I see. In that case, I can sign the release form for you. Don't miss this course next semester.
Melinda: I appreciate it. I will make sure to take this class next semester.

Conversation 2

Jim: Eu-jin, are you taking any classes during the summer session?
Eu-jin: Yeah, I have to take one or two courses.

Jim: So, have you decided which courses you're taking?
Eu-jin: I'm thinking about doing the Master of Linguistics program this fall, so I need to take two more prerequisite courses. Perhaps Second Language Acquisition II and Syntax II.
Jim: Sounds like it's going be a hard summer for you.
Eu-jin: Yeah, how about you, Jim? Are you taking any coures?
Jim: I'll take Biochemistry 300 again. I failed it last year. So, to graduate next spring, I need to pass that biochemistry class.
Eu-jin: You can do it. Good luck!

Conversation 3

(on the phone)
Martin: Sue, how many credits are you taking this semester?
Sue: I'm thinking of taking 12 credits. How about you, Martin?
Martin: I need to take 15 credits because I failed Calculus II last semester. So I have to re-take that course.
Sue: Oh, I'm sorry. You must have a heavy workload.
Martin: Yeah, I know, but I have no other choice. Have you completed your general education requirements?
Sue: Fortunately, yes! Haven't you?
Martin: I still have one more left. I need to take one humanities course. I'm thinking of taking Psychology 101 this semester. Then I'll be done.

Let's do it 2

B. What do these people want to do? Listen to people talking about their study plans and fill in the blanks.

Conversation 1

Ashley: Ryan, have you decided what you want to do after high school graduation?
Ryan: Yeah, I want to go to a vocational school to get a certificate.
Ashley: Sounds great! Which certification do you want to get?
Ryan: I'd like to be an automobile technician, so I need an engineering certification. How about you, Ashley? What are you going to do after graduation?
Ashley: I'm applying to a few universities.
Ryan: What do you want to study?
Ashley: I'd like to study economics.
Ryan: Oh, that sounds tough. What kind of a job do you want to get when you're done studying?
Ashley: I've always wanted to be a stockbroker, so I'll apply at an investment firm.
Ryan: That's cool!

Conversation 2

Mark: Hi, Christina. How are you?
Christina: I'm good. How about you, Mark? You look worried, though.
Mark: Actually, I'm thinking about going back to school. You know I'm a recent high school graduate.
Christina: Why? I thought you were satisfied with your job now.
Mark: I am, but I'd like to study more to improve my chances of being promoted.
Christina: If you can do it, it's really worth it. Just go for it! What do you want to study at university?
Mark: I want to major in sociology. By the way, how's university life?
Christina: It's pretty good, but I don't like my major, so I am thinking of switching my majors.
Mark: To which major?
Christina: Currently, my major is accounting, but I'm thinking of transferring to business management.

Conversation 3

Jason: Hi, Kelly. Long time no see.
Kelly: Hi, Jason. What are you doing here?
Jason: I'm thinking about transferring to this university. I want to get a 4-yerar degree.
Kelly: Oh, I see. What do you do now?
Jason: I go to a community college nearby and I'm taking computer science. But, I want to get a BS degree in order to work in an actual field with better treatment.
Kelly: I think that's a good idea. This university's computer science department has a good reputation.
Jason: Yeah, I heard about that. So, what do you study here?
Kelly: I'm an early childhood education senior.
Jason: Wow! A senior? Time flies so fast! So, what do you want to do after you graduate?
Kelly: I'd like to go to graduate school.
Jason: You want to get a master's degree? Wow, great.
Kelly: Well, it's just a start. I eventually want to go for a Ph.D so that I can become a professor in this university.